INTELLIGENCE RISING

RISING

From Instinct to Intelligence
to Super Intelligence

JOHN DERVIN

iUniverse, Inc.
New York   Bloomington

INTELLIGENCE RISING
From Instinct to Intelligence to Super Intelligence

iUniverse books may be ordered through booksellers or by contacting:

iUniverse
1663 Liberty Drive
Bloomington, IN 47403
www.iuniverse.com
1-800-Authors (1-800-288-4677)

ISBN: 978-1-4502-2338-6 (pbk)
ISBN: 978-1-4502-2339-3 (ebk)

Printed in the United States of America
iUniverse rev. date: 7/20/2010

"The integrative processing and profound analysis of life and its emergent intelligence presented here by John Dervin, PhD, is an expression of his own ongoing evolutionary journey and one that we all must make. His work penetrates and perfuses the core of being." **R.V. Radin, M.D., Practicing Psychiatrist, Vero Beach, Fl.**

"In this provocative analysis of the relationship of human intelligence to cosmic evolution, Dr. Dervin has produced a worthy follow-up to his fine earlier volume, From the Big Bang to the Big Brain." **Philip Eschbach, Professor Emeritus, Broward College, Fl.**

"For many years I have known John Dervin as a very good tennis player. Now it is apparent that he is equally adept as a researcher and writer. His perspective on the evolutionary history of intelligence and its potential for future development is unique and enlightening." **Bill Nichols, Professional Teacher and Head Tennis Coach, University of Nebraska, Omaha.**

"In clear and articulate fashion, Dr. Dervin reviews what we now know about the universe and describes how that knowledge suggests that all relationships, from the furthest galaxy interactions to our most private thoughts, are an interconnected unit. *Intelligence Rising* has the rare combination of being broadly informative and, at the same time, a delight to read. I heartily recommend it on both counts." **Norris Finlayson, M.D., Clinical Professor of Pathology, University of California, San Francisco.**

Contents

ACKNOWLEDGEMENTS

As much as I might wish it to be otherwise, I must admit to being neither research scientist performing fundamental work to advance the leading edge of knowledge nor an applied scientist converting new ideas into technological innovations. As a science writer I work with information garnered from the above two groups. Some among the first group write well but pure science, not writing, is their passion. There is another group of scientists, somewhat removed from basic research, who nevertheless understand the mathematics and theorems and do a good job of translating scientific concepts into the English language. My information is distilled mainly from this latter group and written in the hope of making it a little more reader-friendly on the premise that if I can understand some of these concepts you can too.

In so doing I have relied upon the writing of the select group of authors cited in the bibliography. When direct quotes or close paraphrasing is used I note the originator's name in the text. So as to facilitate the flow of reading, I have not used in-text references.

PREFACE

This is the second book in a trilogy that explores the current status and future prospects for an evolving humanity in an evolving cosmos. In a prior work (*From the Big bang to the Big Brain*) we swept across 14 billion years of cosmic history compacted in a couple hundred pages to discover how only recently, in evolutionary time, our species has emerged on a fresh "young" planet called Earth. Now, as we become more aware of our own inner evolutionary drives, we begin, albeit tentatively, to allow our psyches to expand and merge with the larger processes of cosmic evolution. Increasingly, we are aware that the Darwinian imperative to survive as a species has been realized and we have arrived at an evolutionary juncture where many humans are aspiring to move beyond the slowness of biological evolution and into the realm of expanding the mind. Darwin has provided a rough outline for the physical development of the various species but his explanations are narrowly limited and can take us only so far when we consider the larger aspects of cosmic evolution and the expansion of mind. The time has come to look at findings coming from the new sciences of chaos, complexity, cognitive psychology, and metaphysics. From this group of leading-edge thinkers a trail will be blazed into new conceptual territory and lead us to higher forms of consciousness and the further evolution of the human intellect. An internal drive is emerging within the breasts of humans to transcend the trappings of an ego-dominated existence and to seek discovery of a new human identity. This is evolution in action. We see this broader picture of evolution in the universe as it marches toward increased complexity and as we experience in ourselves a compulsion to seek greater intellectual awareness.

Science gives the broad dimensions, if not all of the details, of how the big bang created those early dusty swirls of sub-atomic particles that found a way to combine and make themselves into galaxies, stars, and planets. Then, in the ultra-hot cooking chambers of these early stars the vital elements needed for life were created. Gigantic supernovae blasted the newly created elements from the searing cores of stars out into space where once again they would swirl, gather, and form new stars with planets. In the universe's unremitting drive to produce complexity, these star-created elements compounded and rose up from the mineral-rich crust of an obscure planet called Earth. Thus began the molecular and cellular combinations that led to life. Not content with simple life forms, a cosmic-wide hunger to increase complexity in physical and biological arrangements began working its magic on planet Earth by organizing tiny cells into small living organisms and eventually into physical bodies with brains.

Intelligence is the attribute that uniquely defines the human species. The phenomenon of intelligence underlies the acquisition of our knowledge about how these events have come about. It has shaped the arts, literature, science, and the very cultural environment within which we now almost exclusively spend our lives. As this inquiry proceeds, many of the traditional concepts of individual intelligence will be challenged by new interpretations from a variety of fields. The deeper origins of the mystifying characteristics of mind and intelligence will be investigated. Conventional wisdom states that individual human intelligence results from the activities of neurons within the brain. Now mounting evidence, much of it from quantum physics and other new fields of inquiry, is demonstrating that the human brain is not an isolated, stand-alone device but rather an integrated component in a universe that is a single, unified system of intelligence in which all parts are interactively connected. This connectivity is especially applicable to the complex patterns in the human brain where electrified neural networks not only process sensory inputs but also resonate with external fields of flowing energy and intelligence in the quantum (q) world.

The position taken here is that intelligence, mind, and consciousness arise not solely from the activities of neurons in an isolated chunk of brain matter. Rather, the human brain, in addition to the processing of information from our sense organs, is increasingly acquiring an ability to tune into the higher frequencies emanating from a q-world laden with intelligence. The clarity of individual intelligence, then, depends on the quality of resonance in the connection between the neural networks in the brain and the cosmic-wide intelligence fields of the q-world.

We begin with an overview of some of the newest concepts that underpin the idea that we live within a surrounding sea of flowing energy, order, and intelligence. This encompassing envelope of flowing energized intelligence is carried on waveforms. In fact, the very nature of the universe at its most fundamental level is a vast ocean of quantum waves whose cosmic mission is to distribute energy and information. And it is accessible to us.

Our physical senses are tuned to perceive only those waves in a narrow band of the electromagnetic spectrum that we call *light* and *sound*. All of the colors and shapes we *see* in the world result from transformations made inside the brain of this limited range of electromagnetic wave energy. Sound waves, too, are converted into information and stored as knowledge in brain circuits. The brain functions by making sense out of patterns of small electrical waves that propagate from neuron to neuron. As these neuronal patterns become stronger and more complex, experience accumulates and conscious awareness and intelligence increase. In the simplest of terms, our senses pick up waves from the outside world and process them by making a new set of waves inside the brain. All we know are waves. And all that exists in the outside world is waves.

In a very real sense, we are a continuation of the evolutionary process that commenced with the birth of the universe. The innate inclination for complexity that prevails throughout the universe is now continuing its evolutionary drive via the brain waves that we interpret as consciousness and intelligence. In us, the universe has created self-reflective beings capable of observing and participating in the evolutionary process. Our evolving intelligence continues as an integral component of the ongoing cosmic processes that commenced with the big bang.

Where is it all leading? We know there is a certain confliction between the material and the nonmaterial, between matter and spirit, that each of us feels in that personal inner world comprised of our intellect. We are not alone in this paradoxical game of confliction at the currently incomplete place in the ongoing process of evolution. In the material world there is the unceasing struggle between entropy and order. In the religious world there is the ever-present tussle between good and evil. In psychology there are contradictory left-brain and right-brain responses and oftentimes indecision between cerebral and emotional choices, between the brain and the heart. There is a long-unresolved tension between science and religion. Each seeks to define human nature and to be the reservoir of truth. And in the lives of many, as we seek the correct path to follow, there is a confliction of choice between intellect and emotion, between reason and intuition, between rationality and inspiration.

Implicit in all that follows is the realization that while these conflictions appear to be real, ultimately they are mere temporary illusions. In the final reckoning, science and religion will circle around and meet each other in the wholeness of a truth greater than the sum of their individual contributions. Left and right brain divisions will better integrate rational thought in a new creative intelligence superior to either reason or inspiration alone.

The subject matter at hand is human intelligence, its origins, its past, and its future trajectories. This approach to intelligence will attempt to move beyond traditional academic dogma and to explore eclectically certain emerging concepts from scientific research along with some of the new systems of thought not currently contained in traditional psychology. We will visit the old positions and propose how promising new ideas have the potential to combine into a coherent synthesis and resolve current conflictions. Three themes will override this treatise and dog its pages throughout:

- Evolution occurs in a broad cosmic sense far beyond the biological confines of Darwinism.
- Intelligence is perceived in a cosmic-wide sense but also can be narrowed down to its manifestations at the human level.
- The human brain is not a stand-alone device but is connected to a universal matrix of intelligence.

A WORLD IN PROCESS

A MARCH TOWARD MIND

It started with a bang. The big bang! And after eons evolving here on Earth, we find ourselves firmly ensconced within the cosmic cradle of *spacetime*. Though constrained by the one-way march of time, confined by physical limitations of natural law, and not really sure where we came from or where we are going, we must proceed.

Before the big bang there was neither space nor time, at least not as we now know them. Anyway that is what the best scientific minds tell us; fact is, we know nothing about the realm outside our universe that preceded the big bang. However, with the onset of the big bang space opened, time flowed, and the evolution of material complexity began.

Immediately following the big bang, the process of evolution began its developmental activities by combining tiny particles of matter. Atoms merged with atoms and soon were forming molecules. The zeal of the evolutionary process to reach for increasing complexity continued its march until molecules formed cells and in time these inanimate cells crossed the critical threshold to become tiny living entities.

To enable this occurrence, the natural laws of charge, force and energy joined to form matter in evermore intricate arrangements making a universe where in time on one planet, at least, the rare event of life occurred. After eons of slow development in the water, muck and mud of a humble planet called Earth, aided and abetted by the sun's radiant energy and perhaps supercharged by bolts of lightning, a few molecules coupled to start the inexorable march toward *life*. Slowly, molecules joined and rejoined, combined and recombined until finally a single-celled entity appeared with the rudimentary features we recognize as *life*. Inanimate matter had complexified and initiated the long upscale journey toward higher forms of life. At some point in this evolutionary process, cellular recombinations were identified as the act of mating, a mere extension of the mysterious early attraction of tiny particles of matter for each other. Continuing with this tendency to merge, and make more complex cellular arrangements, living entities appeared. In time, bundles of brain cells became organized in intricate networks that enabled the birth of the life-preserving attribute of instinct, soon to be followed by the important adjunct of intelligence.

This process has proceeded under the auspices of natural law, which can be thought of as the software package instilled in the universe at the beginning of time. These universal rules of operation guided the formation of matter in the direction of life as unremittingly as imbedded software directs the operation of your computer toward a specified output. It is only natural then to ask the source of this intelligent set of laws. More will be said later about some of the proposed explanations for how natural law originated.

Now, as human intelligence reaches new levels, we are beginning to apprehend the pervasiveness of the phenomenon of consciousness. We are in awe of the power behind its origination and wonder at where this awareness will take us. The earth, our solar system and the entire universe can be thought of as immersed in a huge energy field of intelligence and consciousness. Whether this field is a faint electromagnetic force field or some other still-mysterious energy or quantum field, we are not fully certain. Time will tell as our high-tech instruments grow more sensitive and our own individual awareness gains clearer access to the universal source of this field.

What we do know is that when brains evolve to a sufficiently high level of neuronal complexity, they increase their capacity to tap into this super field of universal intelligence. Across species and within the human species, there is a gradient in the levels of access to this super field and hence levels of individual mental clarity. We are learning that each human brain acts as a focal node through which this larger field of intelligence can pass on information, insight, and a general sense of awareness about self, life, and the world. Continued learning and mental techniques for enhancing awareness can be factors in this process of mind expansion.

Within the processing systems of the brain, there is a mix of information provided by the physical senses with conscious awareness. During our evolutionary development, humanity has slowly become aware first of its nearby surroundings and eventually of the universe in its grandeur. Likewise, following birth, each of us slowly experiences this same awakening of consciousness by apprehending a personal interpretation of the world and our self as a unique instance in the phenomenon of life. Moreover, as humans we are not only aware of this awakening within ourselves but we are aware that we are aware of it. This is the current level of human self-reflective consciousness.

Where do we go from here? It is clear that consciousness, as an inevitable consequence of life, is slowly unfolding both individually and in humanity collectively as a species. As life spiraled upward and gained in complexity, consciousness has emerged to accompany and guide. In our personal lives we can see how, as we become psychologically more complex via normal growth processes and the acquisition of experience, consciousness slowly unfurls. As we learn and grow smarter, the brain increases its capacity by adding new neuronal pathways between brain cells. Much like the stages of physical maturation, levels of consciousness follow a step function as knowledge and insight accumulate. But there are obvious physical limits to the complexity which can occur within the confines of the human brain, fortunately there are features beyond the physical brain waiting to accommodate the continuing expansion of human consciousness and intelligence.

Though there are complexity limitations due to the approximate 1500cc size of the human brain, there is enormous yet-to-developed potential waiting in the wings. As the power of mind increases via growth in brain complexity, there is an amplified ability for gaining access to new levels of intelligence and awareness. The electrical aura surrounding each human body and the chakras (energy centers along the spine) act as interface between the physical and nonphysical. Functioning as an integrated system, the brain, aura, and chakras provide a new and powerful facility for accessing higher frequency levels of consciousness and intelligence.

There are other possibilities for the unrelenting quest by life to advance the growth of intelligence. Think for a minute about the substrate provided by individual brain cells that function as the building blocks for the information processing device we call the human brain. Information passes between these individual brain cells via electrical and chemical signals that follow neuronal pathways created by learning and experience. Now, extrapolate this model to one with each human brain acting as an individual cell or building block for the next higher-level of brain function. This would be a brain working on a global scale. This is the basis for the concept which some call the noosphere; others refer to it as the Gaia hypothesis.

So, the next step in the relentless march of life on the road leading from simplicity to complexity, from individual to cosmic consciousness may be to integrate the advances made in our personal awareness with a collective super consciousness.

THE MARCH OF CULTURE

Since the cultural upheaval spawned by World War II, the pace of change in our social and technological society has increased at an accelerating rate. Rapid transformations throughout the world are placing previously unheard of demands upon people to adapt by making personal behavioral changes. Adult personality structures that in earlier times may well have remained stable throughout an entire lifetime are now being stressed by the pressing need to adjust to unsettling changes.

Although the speed of this transformation is unprecedented, change can be accommodated by individuals. We experience progressive stages of development in our personal lives. We advance through a series of stages that are essentially increases of complexity in the way we are organized physiologically and mentally. Lucky for us that both during the evolution of our species and in our personal development as we grow up, we have been preconditioned for adaptation to change. Immersed in a modern world undergoing revolutionary advances, it is now necessary for individuals to adapt or face the consequence of losing contact with the emerging reality. The phenomenon of change overarches virtually every aspect of life but, simplified, it can be looked upon as continuing attempts to develop complexity. Since the birth of the universe with the big bang and its opening of space and time, complexity has made an unrelenting, upward march. Early creatures have evolved into the wide diversity of life spread across the planet and simple levels of cellular organization have reached the convoluted intricacy found in the human brain. The simple life styles of primitive hunter/gatherer societies have developed into the vast cultural mosaic of the modern world. Changes that formerly required thousands or even millions of years are now time-compressed into much briefer intervals. That the changes occurring around us are coming at an ever-increasing pace can be seen with a quick glance at the table on the next page.

YEARS AGO (approx)	EVENT
14.5 BILLION	THE BIG BANG
4.5 BILLION	SOLAR SYSTEM
3.5 BILLION	FIRST LIFE
65 MILLION	DINOSAURS EXPIRE
7 MILLION	EARLY HOMO.
2.5 MILLION	STONE TOOLS
1 MILLION	USE OF FIRE
135,000 to 34,000	NEANDERTHALS
35,000	CAVE ART
12,000	AGRICULTURE
6,000	WRITING
125	AIRPLANES
75	SPACE EXPLORATION

Looming on the not-too-distant horizon is a new paradigm that will re-define our interpretation of the world we live in. The laws of Newtonian forces and motion have served us well for several centuries but now discoveries from relativity and quantum physics are revealing a more fundamental reality underlying the material world. Physical objects, and even our own bodies at their most basic level, are not at all like they appear to our senses. To enter this new world it will be necessary to embrace some unfamiliar ideas, ideas that may make us uncomfortable because they differ radically from our current view of the world. However, as science advances our understanding of nature, there comes a time when the dominance of old ideas over the existing worldview must be released. The old concepts need not be discarded completely; it is just that they have provided an incomplete understanding of the world.

Nature itself does not discard its earlier work but uses a similar step-by-step building process. For instance, consider the evolutionary development of the tri-partite human brain. As the world became more complex and the small node at the top of the spinal cord no longer served the survival needs of primitive life forms, nature did not abandon out-of-hand its first attempt to achieve perceptive intelligence. When the reptilian brain could no longer accommodate further biological development, evolution added on a limbic system to provide early mammals with increased intelligence for managing body functions and monitoring the environment. A little later nature took another step up the complexity ladder when it surrounded these two older brains with a layer of cerebral cortex. This provided primates with a new ability to process more information and opened the new mental vistas of imagination and abstract thinking.

Hence, the modern human brain consists of three separate but interactive modules. The most ancient of these, known as the reptilian complex, continues to serve our survival needs by imparting automated, instinctive behavior. The limbic system improved on this by introducing the beginnings of emotion and an increased ability to sense both inner and outer environments. And finally for primates, an outer layer of cortex was wrapped around the two older brain modules. Particularly in humans, this cerebral addition produces heightened levels of ability for intelligence, language, and states of awareness.

The point is that these evolutionary advances were accomplished not by doggedly holding on to the status quo or even by discarding older features. Improvements were made by adding enhancements to existing functions. In the case of the human tri-partite brain, the three anatomically dissimilar brain structures combine to form a brain system where, for most run-of-the-mill events, the newer and more advanced parts exert downward control over older more primitive ones. However, there are times as in life-threatening situations when the automated responses of the old survival-oriented reptilian brain may re-assume dominance over behavior.

By folding this style of developmental thinking into past cultural paradigm shifts, we can understand that our current worldview came into existence to replace an earlier, outmoded one and recognize that now the winds of change are portending yet another shift. With the onset of science a few centuries ago, our consciousness moved beyond a geocentric worldview to one that included the earth as one of a system of planets in a universe replete with billions of stars similar to our sun. Then, new laws of force, motion, and gravity, along with the evolutionary theories of biological life entered public consciousness. Now, more recent advances are moving us beyond the old

Newtonian physics and Darwinian evolution of the last century and into newer realms of thought emphasizing relativity, quantum physics, and chaos theory. When new concepts develop to describe how the world functions, the implications for an updated worldview become apparent. As these innovating ways of understanding nature and natural law are able to permeate our current thought patterns more thoroughly, an updated view of our place in the world will come to dominate public consciousness and once again the paradigm will shift.

While the current paradigm is shifting and society is becoming more complex, there is an increasing information load placed on those individuals who wish to compete and prosper. This challenge is reflected in the brain by demands for more neural connections between brain cells. The result is more neural complexity and over time new increases in intelligence. The notion that mental capacity can expand, even in mature adults, is finding substantiation coming from recent research in neuroscience. Surprisingly, there are stem cells in the brain ready to answer rigorous mental challenges by creating new neurons. More on this later but for now suffice to say this is another evolutionary instance where growth results from a focused response to new challenges.

More and more in this evolving cultural context, the way we conceptualize intelligence is changing. Now it can be viewed more as a dynamic, evolving attribute with an innate potential for development throughout an entire lifetime. Early in life intelligence is undeveloped and evolves methodically through stages of increasing complexity. It absorbs and stores the learning and knowledge of one stage as it waits for sufficient momentum to unfold the next step in the maturation process. Now we are learning that intelligence need not be unchanging once the traditional stages of human growth are completed. Transcendence to new levels of awareness and intelligence is not automatic or easy to achieve but there is growing scientific evidence for the brain's ability to create new brain structures and functions in response to mental challenges. The secret for success in this process lies in engaging and coping with mental challenges. Problems do not necessarily need to be solved, only responded to with mindful coping.

A NEW WORLD VIEW

Typically, there has been a close correspondence between the current theories in science, particularly physics, and the dominant worldview concerning the nature of reality. Even when it is not consciously articulated, there is an implicit correspondence between the prevailing worldview and the way we think, use language, create art, and picture ourselves. For many years science professed and followed an atomistic approach in the study of the universe. It was a line of attack in which objects and humans alike were explained by a process of analysis, a breaking down of larger components into smaller pieces for detailed study. The tiny atom was the holy grail. By reducing everything down to basic atomic building blocks, it was assumed higher functions could be understood. For example, it was believed that the operation of the brain could be understood by analyzing the individual structures and functions of the brain. This approach was pursued even down to the level of the neuron. Even Freud at one point in his productive career said that in time the study of human behavior would be reduced to the laws of physics and chemistry. Many of his metaphors used examples from classical physics, the prevailing science of his day.

Following this era of scientific reductionism, brought on by the overwhelming successes of Newtonian physics, the ideas of relativity and quantum physics moved out of the research lab and began to enter the collective consciousness. Slowly this would modify the worldview. The atom was shown not to be the primary constituent of matter but was itself composed of smaller parts. Moreover, when viewed under sufficient magnification these components of the atom behaved more like waves of energy than actual particles of matter. Einstein demonstrated that matter was merely captured energy ($E=MC^2$) and soon, with further revelations from quantum physics, scientists were forced to modify their love affair with analytical thinking, determinism and precise experimental results. Researchers were forced by these radical findings to make peace with an indeterminate subatomic world connected at its foundation by nothing more than waves of energy carrying information. Open chaotic systems and their unpredictable outcomes entered the research domain and had to be dealt with. No longer could the world be viewed as composed of basic building blocks of matter or as objects separated in time and space. Rather, we now had to make peace with the new idea that the universe at its most basic level was a flowing field of energy, information, and intelligence. All of the world's parts and systems combine to form a single dynamic process unfolding in a state of *becoming*. From weather patterns to biological growth, it became apparent that natural events are characterized by an all-encompassing *flow* of energy that connects every thing to every other thing. It began to appear that physics was backing up what philosophers mean when they say, *We are One.*

Quantum theory has not only challenged the old fragmentary view of the world but it converts human beings into participants in the process of cosmic development, much as a researcher in a quantum physics experiment becomes a participant in the ongoing events of a research project. (Strangely, the behavior of particles in the subatomic world is influenced by the consciousness of an observer.) Our view of the world is being irretrievably impacted by these revelations from quantum physics and by other new ideas coming from chaos and open systems theory. We are beginning to understand that there are laws of self-organization at work in nature and that these laws enable a step-by-step evolution to greater levels of complexity. Evolutionary biology is gaining recognition as a more insightful representative of reality than Newtonian physics. What happens within open systems seems to better depict the true nature of living beings than does attempting to understand the brain by analyzing it down to the level of neurons. It is becoming necessary to consider the behavior of totalities rather than subdividing and studying separate parts in a system.

Physicist David Bohm expressed ideas about how the explicate, or visible, world of matter flows out of the invisible, or implicate, world of quantum activity. His ideas have merged with the complexity-formation concepts of chaos and systems theory and this has led to a radically different view of how the world works. This new reality presents us with a picture of the world as a unified whole characterized by an unending flow of energy. There is no separation, no fragmentation; everything is connected. Matter and mind are not discontinuous, only distinct aspects of the same flowing energetic process. In his own words, Bohm's interpretation of nature is best expressed as, "*...all is in an unbroken and undivided whole movement.*" This presents a reality view markedly different from the analytical approach of an earlier world in which objects and creatures were seen as separate and unconnected. Now the emphasis has shifted away from focusing on individual parts to observing how the interactivity of a system's parts can create new functions at the top system level. Performance not seen in any of the components will appear as a radically new outcome at the next higher system level. Evolutionary possibilities and emergent properties in chaotic, open systems have become relevant in science and everyday life. Open systems possess the surprising potential to take in energy, self-organize, innovate, and create something altogether new. Unstable chaotic systems can put one and one together and under the right circumstances the result will be something greater than two. In other words, two components can be connected in a system and produce behavior not seen in either of the two components.

Before attempting to provide a new perspective on the development of intelligence, a look must be taken at the growth process itself; that is, how change takes place not only in the world at large but most especially at the human level. Comprehending how growth in nature has maneuvered its way from simple beginnings to the complexities of today will enable a better understanding of how it was possible for primitive instincts to move across millions of years and hundreds of species to reach the high levels of mentation seen in the modern human brain. And looking beyond the current mental levels in modern H. sapiens, we turn our eyes to new possibilities from the realm of evolutionary change.

THE BEGINNING

The big bang can be thought of as the moment that creation begins. Prior to the big bang, according to the best scientific minds, the makings of the entire universe were contained in a tiny but incredibly dense seed, known as the Singularity. We have demonstrated the unbelievable power contained in the tiny atom. A second weak comparison to the Singularity is the emergence of a giant oak tree from the small seed of an acorn[i]. The Singularity was a point of infinite density, totally lacking space and holding all of the energy that would over time evolve into matter and the magnificent structure that is today's universe.

From the time of Aristotle until 1929, the prevailing view of the world was one of an infinite but static universe, without beginning or end. Even Einstein, though his theorems told him otherwise, could not free himself of the dominance by the overwhelming cultural belief of that time that we live in universe whose stars and

---

i   Even more startling is that the largest living entity on planet Earth, the colossal redwood tree, springs from a seed weighing 1/7400 of an ounce.

galaxies are fixed in space.[ii] Then Hubble, the astronomer not the spacecraft, made a curious discovery that would change our view of the world forever. Much to his own surprise, Hubble found that the galaxies in the universe were moving away from each other. In other words, the universe is not static but dynamic, not stationary but expanding. When other scientists verified this stunning conclusion, a new explanatory model of the world was needed. No longer was it necessary to think of the universe as infinite. If the universe is currently expanding, then by mentally reversing the reel of time all the galaxies can be visualized as re-approaching each other in a contracting universe. As this mental image of the universe returns to time zero, all matter would once again reach a space-less point of physical unity in a new Singularity. So until the next scientific revision, the explanatory model that best describes the beginning point and ensuing elaboration of an expanding universe has come to known as the big bang theory.

For a mental graphic to approximate an image of the big bang, think of a ball with an explosive core surrounded by a number of tightly compressed, tiny pellets. If the ball is hurled high and explodes, the pellets will fly in all directions from the center of the ball and progressively move away from each other. The flying pellets would be

---

ii   When his theorems did not fit the currently-held static model of the universe, Einstein introduced his cosmological constant to make the necessary corrections. Later when it was shown that the universe is actually expanding, the original theorems proved to be correct and the cosmological constant was no longer needed. Einstein called this the biggest blunder of his career.

analogous to the many rapidly diverging galaxies formed from the explosive release of subatomic particles by the big bang. At this point, time commenced, space opened, and the universe unfolded. However, like all analogies this one should not be taken too literally. In the example with the pellets, there is the prior existence of space into which the ball moves and then expels its matter. The analogy is only a rough graphic and not fully accurate because it was only with the onset of the big bang that space opened.

With the simultaneous opening of space and time, subatomic particles of matter hurled forth and mysteriously began to join and build the physical universe. Dusty particles swirled, coalesced and, because of some yet-to-be-understood law of nature favoring complexity, galaxies resplendent with billions of stars began to form. Inside the searing hot nuclear reactors at the center of these stars, new elements were created. In the course of time, stars explode in a supernova and spew their newly formed elements into space leading to the formation of new stars and their planetary systems. Now, however, these stars and their planets are richly endowed new elements, many essential to the formation of life. And on one such planet these very same elements created within stars began to rise up from the rich crust of planet Earth and form the life that would in time become us. We are just as much a result of the universal process of evolution that started with the big bang as is the cosmos itself.[iii]

THE UNIVERSE

So the big bang is creating a universe for us to live in but how do we get our mental arms around a structure so colossal that its dimensions yield only reluctantly even to measurements in light years. Light is the fastest traveler in the universe. A beam of light will circle the Earth seven times in one second. One light year is the distance light will travel in a year's worth of time as it moves at a speed of 186,000 miles per second, or more than five trillion miles per year. The known universe is many billions of light years across and still expanding.

We are going to look at a few of the recent innovations in thinking about the nature of the universe. In particular we want to see how the theories of relativity, chaos, and quantum physics impinge upon our current views of intelligence. To take full advantage of these revelatory insights will require a fundamental shift in traditional thought about how the universe works. Einstein's brainwaves were father to many of these changes. His special theory of relativity postulates that the speed of light is constant regardless of motion on the part of the observer. This law of nature says that whether you are traveling in the same direction as light or moving in an opposite one, the measured speed of light will always

iii   It is interesting to note that to date scientists have identified for certain 108 elements. Of these 108 elements, 90 have been found in the human body and brain and it may well be that the remaining 18 are there yet to be discovered. Only humans have this large total, illustrating the rising of organized complexity in the evolution of the species.

be186,000 miles per second (C). This is critical since everything in the universe is in motion. There are no fixed points. Hence, if you are traveling at 1000 miles per hour and measure the speed of a light shining forward from the front of your craft, the speed of that light will be C, not C+1000 miles per hour. The same is true for a light moving from the back of your craft; its speed will remain C, not C-1000 miles per hour.

Another counterintuitive result of Einstein's work led to our understanding of the equivalence of mass and energy, as defined by the ubiquitous formula $E=MC^2$, where energy equals mass times the speed of light squared. This equation tells us that a small amount of mass contains an enormous amount of energy, as can be appreciated in the tremendous release of energy when the tiny nucleus of a uranium atom is split.

As Einstein followed where his theorems led, he experienced increasing problems with Newton's theory of gravity. It led him to conclude in his general theory of relativity that space and time are intimately wedded throughout the universe and even more surprisingly that spacetime is curved. He explained this novel concept of curvature in the universe by proposing that the mass and energy of large objects warp the fabric of spacetime, much as a bowling ball might cause a warp or indentation in the fabric of a tightly stretched, somewhat elastic canvas. If a golf ball is then rolled across the canvas near the bowling ball, its path will bend toward the larger object as it passes. This effect is seen when light from a distant star passes near our sun; its path is bent. When an object with less mass moves into the warped field of spacetime surrounding a massive body like our sun, the smaller object can be captured in an orbit around the larger body. Hence, Einstein's theories have augmented some of Newton's work by demonstrating curvatures in spacetime. They have turned what we formerly considered empty space into an active player in the dynamics of the universe. His theories also portended the coming end for the centuries-old concept of a static universe. No longer could the universe be considered as having been created in its present-day form. If the galaxies are speeding away from each other, it means that earlier in time they were closer to one another. Running this scenario 14 billion years back in time to the point of the singularity preceding the big bang, space would shrink and density would increase until space disappeared and time was no more.

Unfortunately, when the moment of the big bang is approached, Einstein's theories begin to fail and it becomes necessary for quantum theory to step in to deal with the strange behavior of the micro-miniature particles inhabiting the subatomic realm. Planck was instrumental in advancing the early ideas of quantum physics when he revealed his discovery that when light is emitted it travels in tiny, discrete packages of energy called *quanta*. Later, Heisenberg enhanced Planck's work by demonstrating the impossibility for accurate measurement of both the position and speed of subatomic particles at the same time. In other words, when speed is accurately measured by an observer, the simultaneous measurement of position becomes inaccurate. The vice-versa case holds as well. This would become known as the uncertainty principle and sent many Newtonian scientists up the wall. Even before Newton the certainty of observation, measurement and prediction, when in accord with natural law, was the cornerstone of science. With these new discoveries, an unsettling uncertainty and unpredictability appeared. Indeterminate outcomes entered scientific investigations and open-ended results had to be acknowledged as part and parcel of nature itself. It portended the need for an updated and more accurate worldview, one that encompassed the fluctuations of chaos and open systems and their strange power to self-organize and evolve new levels of complexity. With chaotic systems, it portended an openness of outcomes that could not be predicted in advance and that under certain conditions would create a new result.

Since the advent of relativity, dealing with large objects, and quantum theory, dealing with the microworld, science has attempted to resolve the incompatibility of these two major systems of thought. The goal is to arrive at a single unified *theory of everything*. Only slowly does nature release her mysteries to mere mortals, hence the task of understanding the universe we live in goes on. Some of the recent attempts by the wondrous minds of Stephen Hawking and scientists of his ilk involve the strange and mysterious ideas of black holes, superstrings, ten-dimensional membranes, and eleven-dimensional super gravity. These notions are beyond the pale of this book but the interested reader can consult the bibliography for additional information on these subjects. The upshot of these new insights into the nature of the universe and our role in it means that it is time to look beyond traditional definitions of mind and intelligence. A new vision is needed that incorporates the potential for further development of intelligence is needed.

OPEN SYSTEMS AND INTELLIGENCE

In a previous section, it was pointed out that the paradigm, or mental model, we humans use to help us interpret natural and social events, is currently in the process of shifting away from dominance by the physical sciences. In the past emphasis has been on analysis and materialism but now there is movement toward the more holistic approach of the life sciences. The new view is not yet fully accepted in certain sectors of science but slowly the wide applicability of concepts from systems theory and evolutionary biology are gaining recognition. They represent more insightful and accurate descriptions of the world we live in. Fundamental realities of nature seem to be more poignantly depicted by the recent interpretations coming from quantum theory, chaos, and open systems than by analytical reduction and the straight-line thinking of Newtonian physics.

Many of the novel concepts from these new arenas of thought are a natural fit for biology and studies in the evolution of life. After all, living organisms are open systems. In a biological sense, individual organisms do not evolve, except in the sense that they can temporarily reverse the effects of entropy by learning and personal growth. But in the Darwinian sense, populations of individuals do evolve. Those individuals best suited to their particular environment have a greater influence on the gene pool by living longer than the less fit and passing their genes on to more offspring. In this way, biological populations slowly change in response to the survival dictates of their habitat.

When a population becomes isolated from others of its kind, the changes brought about in the isolated group by their new environment (if that environment is somewhat different from the old one) can become large enough to create a new species. This is part of the explanation for how over eons of time the enormous ecological diversity around the world, coupled with genetic variability, has elicited from life's simple beginnings the great biological variety seen on this planet. It explains how genetic variability and the demands of new environments have drawn out the various physical and mental attributes that best enable survival in a particular environmental setting. Relying on an innate potential to respond to the great variety of environmental demands, species have emphasized fang, claw, speed, or sheer size as their survival tools. Others have relied upon cunning, social organization, and incremental levels of intelligence as their attribute of choice for survival.

Attending the processes of evolution, and assisting our understanding of it, are the newly recognized principles of chaos and self-organizing systems. Whatever may be the source of actions operating in open systems, these systems help in defining the *how* and *why* behind the pervasive evolutionary processes bringing about molecular and biological complexity. Because of the self-organizing actions taking place in open systems, and possibly along with other unifying principles, life has gained order and organizational complexity while moving from single cell organisms to the intricate grouping of a trillion-plus cells in human beings.

For evolution to work its "magic," there must be at least three processes at work. Together, they mediate the interactions between living organisms and their eco-sociological niche. The first two are the usual ones cited by Darwinists.

- Genetic variation within populations such that physical and mental characteristics vary slightly from parents to offspring.
- Natural selection by the environment of those physical and mental variations that favor survival, enhance chances for reproduction, and lead to improvement of the species.

The third is still under study by chaos and open systems theorists but it is charged with potential:

- Intense periods of evolutionary change resembling the high-energy fluctuations of chaotic open systems. These brief intervals often result in a creative breakthrough and a more viable adaptation. Examples would be when early hominids first split off from a more apelike ancestral line or when brain size, and hence intelligence, made the critical leaps from Australopithecus to H. habilis to H. erectus to H. sapiens.

We may now be nearing the next evolutionary advance that will accommodate yet another leap in intelligence.

THE FIRST FAMILY

With this rudimentary understanding of how evolution in principle works, we can move to an *up close and personal* view of how our distant ancestors separated from other members of the animal kingdom. Do not be discomforted by the misconception that apes became human. The missing link has never been found because there isn't one. There were many divergent steps between ape and human. Once the first group of monkeys diverged, that group followed its own evolutionary path that has led to the diverse crop of monkeys seen today. The same independent developmental schemes are true for the great apes, chimpanzees and the hominids as well. It is true that when you trace the evolutionary descent of these three primate groups (monkey, ape, and hominid) back far enough, the paths do converge in a single line. This indicates a common evolutionary history prior to the points of divergence; hence a distant ancestral relationship. But once the lines diverged, chimps and apes produced only more chimps and apes and the early, small-brained, crudely-bipedal hominids evolved over millions of years into H. sapiens.

Hark back to the discussion of the energetic fluctuations that occur in open systems. Scientists have discovered that within such systems dynamic fluctuations can lead to divergent paths of development. In a dynamic system, diverging paths (bifurcations) do occur and in many cases, if energy continues to pour into the system, a series of bifurcations oftentimes will occur. This is the sum and substance of evolutionary change in open systems. It is the means by which innovation and development reach new and higher levels of order.

It is this process that drives evolution toward increasing complexity.

As more fossilized bones and fragments of teeth are found, a better picture of the physical appearance and lifestyle of early hominids comes into focus. One revelation contrary to accepted belief came about when the notion of "linked evolution" became discredited. Since Darwin's original pronouncements on the subject, most anthropologists had professed that once hominids split off from their ancestral line they were essentially human, possessing from the start the beginnings of their distinguishing human characteristics. Darwin had envisioned a simultaneous development of those attributes which uniquely define humans, i.e., bipedalism, increased brain capacity, tool technology, smaller canine teeth, language, social interaction and culture. Until recently most anthropologists agreed that these distinguishing human traits had evolved in unison. They were seen as acting as a sort of cybernetic feedback system which synergistically enhanced their mutual growth. This was thought to be of particular importance because the demands of tool making and social interaction were seen as feeding the growth of brain capacity. This all seemed very plausible and even credited humans with a clean and decisive break from an embarrassing apelike ancestor.

But it didn't happen that way. Bipedalism occurred first. For some three million years, these early human prototypes worked on improving their upright gait but retained definitive apelike characteristics of a small brain, little in the way of culture, and a social structure very much like that of a modern baboon troop.

Moreover, the somewhat romantic notion of adventuresome hominids swinging down from their arboreal homes and bravely venturing out to meet the challenges of terrestrial life, is also likely in error. As the eastern African climate became cooler and more arid, the most probable scenario is that their habitat changed so imperceptibly that differences were unnoticeable from generation to generation. Over millennia the diminished rainfall slowly changed their two-hundred-foot-high, heavily canopied habitat to one where, on the perimeter at first, smaller trees permitted sunlight to reach the ground and bring forth bushes, grasses, and root vegetables. Without making an intentional exodus from the thickly treed forests and without ever venturing outside their habitat, their home was remodeled. As the environment changed, the selection preference by the environment also changed. New and more adaptive physical characteristics presented by the gene pool were selected. It is likely that several hundred thousand generations of the various Australopithecus species existed during the approximate two million years following their split-off from a more primitive line. The many small physical variations presented by individuals during this long period enabled natural selection to mold Australopithecus into a bipedal, terrestrial athlete. As the trend toward bipedalism progressed, it was supported and encouraged by continued environmental transitions. Woodlands became increasingly sparse and the survival requirements on the ever-widening savanna demanded not only biological adjustments but new mental aptitudes as well. Only the quick and cunning survived. The culling effect of this new, harsher, and more demanding environment placed a new emphasis on brain development and *intelligence.*

As the woodlands became more dispersed, the new environment of an open savanna with its carnivorous big cats and wild dog packs required new adaptive attributes from early hominids. Those who would survive needed a new level of foot speed as well as social cooperation and a cunning intelligence. It is an old story for life on Earth. As climates change and familiar econiches disappear, those creatures with a specialized ability finely tuned to the old environment tend not to be able to make the necessary adjustments to the demands of new conditions. On the other hand, because they have a wider range of skills, those with a more generalized intelligence are better able to adapt to changing conditions. Neocortical advancements in early primates were a consequence of at least three interrelated factors: social interactions, new learning experiences, and diet. For the evolving species of hominids, a broad-based form of generalized intelligence was life's weapon of choice for survival.

ICE CYCLES

With a modified style of movement and a new athleticism firmly established in protohumans, along with an incipient technology for tool making, the next step in the biological evolution of hominids once again would be tied to climatic change. After millions of years of cooler, drier weather in Africa, the gradual formation of massive ice caps at the north pole created a new phenomenon. The result was that several million years ago, rhythmic glaciations began. As ice moved downward into Europe and North America, there was less atmospheric moisture available for rainfall, making Africa even drier and its living conditions more severe. This introduced another permutation in the evolutionary process. An approximate hundred-thousand-year cycle of glacier expansion and recession commenced and was reflected in Africa by long periods of dry, harsh environmental conditions interspersed with shorter periods of warm, wet weather that brought easier living conditions. Had the glaciers not receded periodically, the entire continent of Africa would have become a desert, drastically altering the possibilities for life there. Fortunately for our distant ancestors, the glaciers of Europe and Asia would pull back periodically, ushering in warm wet weather and the lush greenery of interglacial periods would return. As this new climatic pattern emerged, repeating itself over and over every hundred thousand years or so, a new and demanding relationship developed between weather cycles and human evolution. Demanding new challenges to survival placed a selection emphasis on the evolving hominids for better intelligence and increased brain capacity. Soon H. erectus succeeded H. habilis, who had replaced the smaller-brained Australopithecus.

During the periods of maximal glaciations, life in Africa became increasingly severe as vital warmth, rain and vegetation were replaced by cooler, drier conditions. Only the most fit and clever would make it through to the return of the warmth, wetness, and the welcome abundance of the next interglacial period. Then once again, as the ice moved down from the north, there would be a return to the harshness of starvation, predation and death for the less athletic, hardy and cunning. This cycling of ice across the northern latitudes and its stunning effect on the eastern African climate and landscape is thought to be unique in the geological history of the planet. Call it divine manipulation, natural law, Mother Earth's way, or whatever you wish, it was because of these repeating cycles of famine and feast that certain members of early humanity with certain attributes were selected for survival and the right to pass on their genes to subsequent generations. This is a perfect illustration of how coping with challenge can result in growth. In this instance intelligence was the principal beneficiary.

Over time, small increments in brain capacity occurred. Those with the intellectual traits that made them equal to the challenges of the changing environment moved from a creature with an ape-sized brain to one with an incredible three-fold increase in size. After a few million years of this climatic cycling and its uncompromising selection of those genetic variations that would improve brain capacity and intelligence, the biological engineering of the infrastructure for the human brain was complete. This magnitude of change over such a short period of evolutionary time is unprecedented. The English biologist, J.B.S. Haldane, has characterized the brain explosion, and hence intelligence, during the seven-million-year period encompassing Australopithecus, H. habilis, H. erectus and finally the arrival of H. sapiens as the fastest evolutionary transformation known to science.

THE BIG BRAIN ARRIVES

As a marvelous instrument of supremely condensed intricacy, the human brain has inspired wonder and disbelief in scientist and layman alike. With its 100 billion-plus neurons (worms have 23), its storage capacity of 100 trillion memory sites (my PC has 280 million), and neural connections in excess of 10 quadrillion (more than all the electronic network connections on Earth), the mysterious origin and design of the brain's marvelous functions have driven many hard-nosed scientists to reach for metaphysical explanations.

How the early hominid brain moved from the Australopithecine capacity of 450 cc (roughly the size of a chimpanzee brain) to the full capacity of 1400 cc in modern H. sapiens in such a brief period of evolutionary time has been a source of puzzlement to many anthropologists and neuroscientists as well. Alfred Russell Wallace, co-discoverer of the evolutionary theory along with Darwin, could not understand how the early hominid brain continued to grow after it had achieved the necessary size advantage over its competitors. Moreover, the brain maintained its growth trajectory (averaging an increase of 180 cc per million years) until 'suddenly,' in evolutionary time, it had ballooned into modern size. For all intents and purposes, the brain of late H. erectus possessed much of the structure and mental potential of the modern human brain, which ranges from approximately 1000 to 1700 cc. Strangely, the prehistoric brain of H. erectus came with a built-in, pre-adapted potential for such future refinements as abstract thinking, mathematics, art, language and musical composition. The astonishing fact is that this potential was achieved many millennia prior to the rise of a cultural emphasis on such advanced cognitive functions.

From a Darwinian perspective, whether it be tooth, claw, speed of foot, or brain, a particular attribute will be favored if it enhances the likelihood for the gifted parents to produce more offspring than parents with less of the attribute. The genetic code ensures that offspring receive an approximate, though not identical, replication of their parent's biological attributes. Some receive more of an attribute, some less; hence, those with better levels of an attribute (running speed, stealth, intelligence, etc.) than their parents would be in a more favored position to survive, reproduce and so to pass along their genes. Thus, the long progression of selective improvement over millions of years and countless generations moved forward.

Life in its unrelenting quest to endure and prosper has followed many paths, all designed to foster survival. We can see the excellence evolution has achieved in swimming, flying, running, burrowing, fecundity, and the extremes of size from minute to gigantic. Other techniques used to enhance the survival of life can be seen in the heavy protective shell of the turtle, the vast numbers of roe spawned by fish, the poison fang of the snake, the concealing camouflage of certain insects and mammals, and the sly cunning of fox and leopard. These are some of the many diverse steps taken by evolution as it sought a means to ensure that life continued. As it turns out, increased brain size and intelligence were the techniques life chose to ensure the survival of early humanity. (It should be noted that at the level of individuals, intelligence does not necessarily correlate well with brain size. Across species it does.)

In its basic structure, the human brain is not much different from an ape brain. It was not redesigned from scratch for humans, only provided with new additions. Evolution's way is to build upon what it has already created by making small modifications, some of which turn out to be useful and are retained. When enough of these small modifications accumulate, something quite new may appear. The old part of the human brain remains much the same as the ape's. The vital enhancement for H. sapiens was the cerebral cortex, the new convoluted layer of neuronal material that surrounds the outer portions of the old mammalian brain. Aptly, it is called the neocortex.

Operationally, the human brain is quite different from earlier brain models due to add-on functions for processing large amounts of information and the lateralization of the neocortex into functional halves. However, most of our basic drives and emotions emanate from the older parts of the brain. The higher, more cerebral functions are performed in the neocortex, particularly in the greatly enlarged prefrontal lobes. Part of the human condition derives from the fact that there is not an absolute or fool-proof top-down control system within the brain to mediate behavior. In fact, at times there can be a competing struggle for behavioral control between the old emotional drives and the newer information processing functions. One way of viewing well-integrated (civilized) behavior is by the degree of success the higher mental functions have in inhibiting and sublimating the more primitive animal drives and impulses. Civilization can be viewed as a triumph of intelligence over instinct.

THE BRAIN PUZZLE

Some scientists cross over into evolutionary biology in their search to understand how the human mind developed in a natural world. To neuroscientists like Sperry and Eccles it appears that Darwinian evolution can carry the development of brain and mind only so far. Beyond a certain point of development a more comprehensive explanation is needed. Darwinian evolution adequately explains the sensory development of the brain. The processing of sensory information was crucial for survival in the natural world. How to swing accurately from branch to branch without wiping out led to improvement in the visual areas of the brain. How far to jump to clear a stream or ravine was a mathematical calculation and a learning process for the brain. How to cooperate in hunting large, fast or dangerous animals and then to share the rewards led to social intelligence. Many mammals and primates in addition to early humans engaged in these activities and those best at it were selected for survival. But beyond the sensory brain, and in the brain of humanity alone, lies a very different set of abilities.

It is here that hard-nosed scientists holding to a strict scientific methodology get stuck. How do mathematical and musical geniuses perform their mental gymnastics with a brain that acquired its size so early in evolutionary time? How did this early brain back in the pre-historic ice age acquire its potential for undreamed of future mental abstractions? This was a pre-civilized world long before humans forsook their wandering habits and settled down to an agrarian style of life. What would be the survival advantage of acquiring such mental talents during that early time? Recognizing that the biological development of the sensory brain occurred from the demands of a natural habitat, what then propelled the brain's cognitive development so far beyond that point? Why did the cerebral cortex expand to encompass the vast neuronal complexity needed for abstract and creative thinking? Why is there an intellectual curiosity to seek and explain the invisible, non-sensory worlds of cognitive psychology and quantum physics? What led us to investigate and unravel much of the underlying microscopic structure of the cosmos?

Many questions regarding the full evolutionary development of the human brain remain unanswered. How are certain brain/mind phenomena, such as the following, explained from a strict Darwinian perspective of evolution?

- *Untutored, third-world "mathematicians" who write theorems that astound some of the best mathematical minds in the world*
- *Precocious musical geniuses who begin composing at very young ages*
- *"Magical calculators" who have no idea how they do it but can perform massive mathematical functions in their heads or determine the day of the week for a specific date a century or more in the past or future*
- *Mathematicians, artists, and musicians who are driven to develop and practice their art for*

> *its sheer elegance and beauty without regard to*
> *practical (survival) considerations.*

How Darwin himself might explain some of these higher mental faculties is uncertain except that some staunch current-day Darwinians use the "Swiss Army Knife" metaphor to illustrate how earlier brain developments might be recruited under different conditions to perform new functions. Wallace, co-discoverer of the evolutionary theory, alluded to *"...a different agency coming into play in order to develop the higher intellectual and spiritual nature of man."* Clearly, such mental functions were not evolved within the usual context of Darwinian natural selection. We can probably agree that the sensorial brain/mind was developed by means of the evolutionary principles discussed earlier but the rational and intuitive functions of the mind present a more puzzling challenge. If, as the best current information tells us, our brains evolved to near current size by the time H. erectus left Africa to explore and settle the Middle East, Europe and Asia, then we must face the question of how this brain growth came about in the pre-civilized, survival-oriented setting of the African savanna. The primary needs of this era were food-gathering, hunting, averting predation, cooperation with family and group members, and some basic tool making. Did this environmental setting develop the complex brain structures needed to tune in the higher intellectual functions? How do we explain the enigma of a brain consisting of discrete components whose functions are divided, yet strangely coupled? This division is not just between hemispheres but between the original spinal stem and the add-on parts of the brain. Biological evolution adequately explains development of the older sense-oriented parts of the brain, shared by humans with the other primate populations. However, the runaway development of newer, rational, intuitive, and information-processing components unique to humanity remains an interesting enigma. The end result of this incredible cerebral expansion has created a huge culture gap between humanity and the rest of the animal species. This gap is a direct result of the increased cerebral areas of the brain and its accompanying intelligence.

Traditional Darwinian theory cannot be relied upon exclusively to acquire further insight into the mechanics of how the brain may have achieved this prodigious leap in capacity. So it is time to consider the incursion of chaos theory and open systems thinking in evolutionary biology and how self-organizing structures can create novel developments.

After departing their ancestral home in Africa, the stressing effects from dramatic climatic changes caused activation of new genes in the wandering populations. In turn, certain of those mutations elicited improved survival characteristics for early humans. These newly activated genes in the population's gene pool enabled novel biological and behavioral adaptations in the form of better ground mobility, guile, tool and weapon making, hunting techniques, social cooperation, and language. For those inadequately endowed, the inevitable alternative was extinction. But environmental conditions cannot draw out traits that are not already included in the genotype. From whence comes this vast array of possibilities contained in the human genetic code?

It is the claim of strict evolutionists that the immense complexity of the genetic code and the convoluted intricacy of the human brain somehow developed by random chance, or "accident". A trial and error explanation devoid of a set of rules, however, seems to be sorely inadequate to the task of organizing the diverse capacity and intelligence of the genetic code. This suggests that some factor beyond the tenets of Darwinism is at work in the development of mind and indeed in the universe at large.

In spite of a somewhat impreciseness in our ability to define exactly what intelligence is, we cannot leave the subject of brain expansion without mentioning the selective importance of intelligence to survival. As culture and language entered the lives of an evolving humanity, the importance of the physical environment was replaced to a certain extent by a growing cultural environment. Increasingly over time, humans have lived and competed in a social, technical, and economic milieu of their own making. This gave an advantage to those individuals with the mental abilities needed to prosper and proliferate under new and varying circumstances. Just as bipedalism and athleticism were selected in the earlier natural environment on the savanna, a generalized intelligence was now being favored, not just by the new demands of a harsh natural habitat but increasingly by the requirements for success in the cultural environment within which humans lived. As culture developed, innovation provided early humans with more protection from climatic uncertainties. Better shelters, clothing, and the use of fire and tools tendered the security of a comforting buffer that protected from the severities of environmental extremes. So now, the very culture that humans themselves were creating began to select for increased levels of intelligence in populations. It became important for new and improved techniques to be invented and then applied by those who were best suited to use them. There was a slow transition away from an emphasis on sensory intelligence for surviving in the physical environment and toward an emphasis for the more cerebral type of intelligence useful in their cultural environment. Thus, as civilization progressed, humanity increasingly lived within a cultural bubble of its own making.

DARWIN AND DESIGN

We have talked about how the tenets of Darwinian and neoDarwinian theories have been used to explain the diversity of life. These theories adhere to a strict scientific methodology that rejects foresight, planning, prior design or a goal-oriented direction for the path of evolution. They employ randomness to produce various characteristics that are seen as chance-determined by genetic variations. If there is the appearance of design or an intelligent plan at work it is only because the natural habitat selects out those characteristics best suited for survival so they can be passed on to the next generation. The theory aspires to a full scientific explanation without recourse to intervention. Needless to say, those of a strict religious persuasion who count themselves as creationists are in sharp disagreement with this explanation of life, its origin, and goals. In addition to these two groups, there is a cadre of scientists who neither comply fully with traditional Darwinian evolutionary explanations nor are they willing to accept the simplified, nonscientific story offered in creationism.

Certain of the scientists in this latter group see an improbability too great for random chance to have elicited the organizational complexity found in the today's world. Granted that leaving to chance the physical diversity of life is not an easy concession but it is one that many scientists will make. Taking the next step to explain how something as complex as the brain developed its extraordinary powers with its many processing flexibilities and vast potential for abstract thought, creativity, intuition, and expanded levels of consciousness is a far more difficult task. The cosmos aside, and considering only the organizational complexity of the human brain, there is a serious question about the ability of random gene mutation and natural selection by the environment to account fully for the complexities of mind and human intelligence.

To say there is randomness, and hence chance, in the presentation of mutant genes to the environment for selection is one thing. It is quite another to assume that chance performed the prior task of designing the vast intricacy of the genetic code. It is questionable that the environment acting upon random mutations would succeed in producing by chance the creation of such high levels of organization. Admittedly, the environment favored for survival those giraffes with longer necks because of their better feeding opportunities. And it can also be conceded that female peacocks favored males with brighter colors. Hence, today we see how evolution produced long necks and colorful tail feathers. But how do you take the next step and explain what drove the human brain to full physical size some 500,000 years before the existence of civilization. This happened long before the appearance of anything faintly resembling modern culture which appeared some 10,000 years ago. It was only then that a new importance on abstract and creative thinking came into play. Even if we concede this colossal size increase to the workings of natural selection, we are left with the problem of what drove the brain beyond sheer size to a complex instrument with such enormous cognitive capacities. The human brain contains billions of densely packed neurons, incredible excesses of networking between brain cells, and design sophistications like parallel circuitry, lateralization, and both localization and globalization of its many hi-tech functions. The sophisticated organization needed for such mental capabilities seems beyond a construction driven exclusively by random chance and survival instincts. One is left to wonder if there isn't some innate intelligence embedded in the evolutionary system itself. Beyond the two tenets of Darwin, it is becoming apparent there is a third factor performing a silent coercion for evolution to reach for more and more complexity in physical and biological arrangements.

There are many human mental capabilities, now accepted as commonplace, that are well beyond the reach of modern computer technology. The operational efficiency of the brain, for example, is greatly enhanced by its parallel processing circuits. These circuits enable the simultaneous, real-time coordination of incoming sensory information with a database of previously stored knowledge, experience, goals, and emotional states. It is difficult to accept on blind faith that these sophisticated refinements all happened by a long and lucky series of random occurrences. That said, it is not necessary to make a leap beyond nature to a divine form of outside intervention. The developing fields of quantum physics, chaos theory, and self-organizing systems offer promise of a fuller understanding of the marvelous capacities of brain and mind and how they may have evolved. These methodologies introduce an elusive third factor complementing the earlier two tenets of Darwinian theory. This third factor, instilled in natural law and operating since the moment of creation, seeks complexity. Later we will explore the implications of this third evolutionary factor and how research may open a new and radically optimistic view on the potentials for human intelligence. First, a deeper look at the roots of intelligence.

INSTINCT, INTELLIGENCE AND EVOLUTION

To better understand the nature of intelligence and its long evolutionary history, we go back to its beginnings several billion years ago when simple forms of life first began to "sense" information about the outside world. Early life forms this information to guide survival-oriented behavior. Thus began the slow process leading to intelligence.

By knowing something of its past, we can better understand how the development of intelligence connects us with our evolutionary history, how it directs our current behavior, and how it portends future possibilities. In its broadest meaning, intelligence encompasses a variety of terms that range from instinct and intuition to imagination, insight, ingenuity, and information processing. For humans, the abstract reasoning powers of the cerebral cortex singularize our form of intelligence and distinguish us from the rest of earth's creatures.

Across the various species there is a recognizable correlation between intelligence and cranial capacity. In general terms, mice are considered more intelligent than frogs and dogs more intelligent than mice. A more accurate indication of species intelligence incorporates the brain-to-body-weight ratio. Since cranial size is all the fossil record has left as an indicator for the intelligence of fossilized species, this hard evidence shows a clear progression in brain size across species and over time. And in living animal species, neuroscientists have shown that all neurons are about the same size; so an increase in brain mass accommodates an increase in the number of brain cells. A greater number of brain cells indicates more neural networks and this equates with an increase in overall brain complexity resulting in better integration of sensory inputs, more potential for processing incoming information, and ultimately a wider variety of behavioral responses. Hence, increased intelligence is the result.

The current levels of human mentality can be thought of as having begun eons ago when the simplest of cellular organisms developed tiny sensors to extract information from the external environment. These primitive sensing devices enhanced survival by detecting food and light. We might even think of intelligence as existing prior to this when plants would sense and turn toward the energy of sunlight. Eventually, animals would develop spines and resting atop the spinal cord would be a tiny bundle of neural material. Primitive "brains" consisting of just a few neurons were radically different from a modern human brain and its capability for integrating the firing of trillions of neurons, rapid processing of information, and the production of what we now routinely take for granted as normal intelligence. The evolutionary process accomplished this feat by adding new brain structures to old ones. Now we may be on the threshold of integrating another "add-on" to enhance intelligence in the form of the body's surrounding sphere of energy known as the aura. More will be said later about this nascent potential for the enhancement of intelligence.

FROM INSTINCT TO INTELLIGENCE

If we move backward in time from the current large bulbous cranial vault that houses the modern human brain, past the primates and other mammals, past the birds and reptiles and to the simpler creatures preceding them, a point is reached where the brain has diminished in size to a mere nodule at the top end of a spine. At this level, there is little of the information processing and none of the abstract mental formulations routinely done by the human brain. In this early time, wired-in instincts ruled behavior such that a fixed reaction would automatically kick in and elicit a specific behavioral response to a particular sensory stimulus. A good example of how instinct works can be seen in the innate and automatic reaction of a baby chick. It is instantly consumed by fear and runs for the safety of its mother the very first time the shadow of a hawk passes nearby on the ground. No learning or interpretation of the meaning of the sensory input provided by the passing shadow is required. For millions of years instinct sufficed as the directing means for creatures as they responded reflexively to the survival challenges in their environments. However, as more and more organisms evolved greater size and increased complexity, instinct with its automated stimulus-response mechanism was augmented in order to provide a greater variety of behaviors. Versatility of behavior became imperative for staying alive in an increasingly complex and competitive world. Gradually, the sensing mechanisms of sight, hearing, smell, touch and taste improved and collaterally the necessary brain mass needed to process this additional information also slowly increased. No longer was behavior determined exclusively by an instinctive reaction. Intelligence began to intervene between stimulus and response. It was an upgraded, higher-tech means of enhancing survival chances by providing a wider behavioral repertoire that not only could be more appropriate to the situation but would allow responses to be selected by willful intention.

How did intelligence manage to replace instinct without leading to an interim loss of adaptability and possible extinction before the transformation was complete? After all, instinct evolved and worked for a very long time as a survival mechanism for creatures as they interacted with their environments. Intelligence would of necessity have to begin at a primitive level. It could not replace instinct abruptly for it would have been inadequate by itself to provide for the many requirements of survival. Intelligence requires a learning period and an accumulated database of experience to draw upon. At the early stages, there must have been occasional weak interventions by intelligence as it proceeded to gain knowledge and built memory.

Instinct, with its built-in, stereotyped responses had served life well as it progressed on the road to proliferation but there were limitations. The limited variety in responses that an instinctual system could account for meant that only a few situations in a given environment could be handled. What about the unusual? What if the environment changed? The shades, gradients, and variations of non-standard conditions arising in natural and soon in social environments as well were too diverse for the limited number of pre-programmed reactions of an instinctual system. The introduction of an add-on embryonic intelligence system was nature's way of upgrading the old device. It was a gradual replacement accomplished with the new system of intelligence intervening only as it *learned* how to better promote survival. Whereas early instincts allowed only a fixed reaction, such as approach or avoid, intelligence can be thought of as the addition of more flexible responses.

As evolution progressed, organisms were able to time-delay the automatic response to incoming stimuli. It was within this narrow window of opportunity that intelligence developed. Inhibition of basic drives and instincts was key. Of course, this development was enabled only as neuronal growth progressed in the central nervous system. As intelligent behavior took its place in the animal world, trial and error learning entered the mix. Since learning is stored in memory, a data base of information began to accumulate. The result was an ever-increasing memory bank that could be called upon to inhibit instinct in the appropriate situation. As learned refinements in behavior responses improved, intelligence became increasingly important as a player in the game of life.

During the evolutionary process of growth in brain mass and intelligence, the different species developed their sensory and perceptual intelligence in various ways. Varying conditions in environmental niches and different styles of adapting to these niches resulted in an emphasis on different senses and differing behavioral styles. Thus, there are bats that can navigate by sounding out their dark environment. There are subtle communication sounds and signals used in the behavioral interactions of creatures from birds to monkeys and there are highly-organized groups of baboons and wolves that survive because of an intricately-evolved social order. These traits can be viewed as a consequence of intelligence as it elaborated and assisted organisms in their unending search for survival and the quest to move beyond mere survival to conditions of comfort and prosperity.

From our current vantage point, it is deceptively inviting to look retrospectively at brain growth as it developed in simple early creatures, progressed from fish and reptiles to birds, and on to mammals, primates and humans, and then to make the assumption that during its odyssey, intelligence developed in all organisms as a singular entity. This perception assumes an expansion from the very beginning in a linear, one-dimensional manner until reaching a pinnacle in humans. This same mistaken assumption can also be made when considering an increasing brain mass and the accompanying expansion of intelligence across today's phylogenetic hierarchy of living animals. Such a view of intelligence is far from truth since great variety and many specializations of intelligence now exist in the animal kingdom. For the sake of simplicity, it would be convenient to make a second error and assume a linear relationship between brain mass and intelligence; that is, as brain size increases a corresponding positive increase in mental ability should be expected. In very gross terms, where large brain-size differences exist, i.e., snake versus chimpanzee, there is a rough correspondence between size and mental ability. But other factors enter the equation. One important factor is the *ratio* of brain-to-body weight as a determinant for intelligence. This ratio takes into account the necessity to allocate a certain amount of brain matter to the indispensable physiological functions of sensory monitoring, control of the muscles, hormonal activities and digestion. The larger the body, the more brain mass needed for operating and maintaining the basic physiological functions. If this ratio is low, as in amphibians and reptiles, there is little neuronal capacity left over for higher cognitive processes.

In humans, the brain-to body ratio is about four times that of the apes and apes exceed all other mammals. While both the whale and elephant have larger brains in absolute terms than do people, the brain-to-body-weight ratio still very much favors humans. Yet, this still is not the end-all measure for intelligence across the animal species. The mouse and other very small mammals have a ratio of brain size to body weight superior to humans. Still other factors must be considered and chief amongst these is the relative size of certain areas of the brain. If you take the brain of a mouse and inflate its size uniformly to that of a human brain, much as a balloon is inflated, you would not wind up with a human brain either in structure or function. That part of the brain known as the cerebral cortex, and particularly the prefrontal lobes, is disproportionately large in humans. It accounts for much of the high-level cognitive brain functions that are available only after the routine tasks of biological operation and maintenance are met.

To understand the evolutionary relationship between brain growth and intelligence, it helps to understand that as the various species "made a living" in their particular ecological niches, each species' brain organization proceeded in very specialized ways. Not all creatures developed the non-specialized, general intelligence of the human family. For example, the spatial mapping abilities of many animals as they travel over terrain provide navigational skills far superior to humans for this specific task. And the spatial memory of the nutcracker is daunting in its uncanny ability to hide seeds in more than twenty thousand different locations each season and then return, from memory, to more than ten thousand of these hidden sites. Certain animals are natural engineering marvels for nest and dam building, other species sport great diversity in their wily survival behaviors, and still others have acquired highly organized social structures in order to sustain life and limb.

We have a tendency to evaluate the intelligence of animals by a comparison to human intelligence. Rather, we should think of one member's behavior in relation to others of the same species. It well may be that there are wolf geniuses who exist on the far right side of the bell curve for wolf intelligence. A bright and well-adapted wolf would be one exceptionally adept at meeting the natural and social requirements of its environment, not the human one.

Whereas most animals have developed specialized forms of intelligence, enabling their efficient exploitation of one particular econiche, the intelligence evolved by humans is more generalized in its nature. Specialized intelligence provides an effective means of survival for the narrow environment to which it is adapted but it is because of this very proficiency that a sort of successful complacency sets in and retards broader evolutionary development. Thus, sharks, as well-adapted and efficient survivors, have not changed in many millions of years. And the narrowly specialized dinosaurs became extinct when their adaptive niche changed, while at the same time and under the same conditions, the more flexible mammals were able to adapt to the new circumstances, evolve and survive. It was the further evolution of this adaptive flexibility and generalized intelligence that enabled early humans to meet the challenges in the harsh climates of new territories, allowing them to expand into all continents on the planet save the South Pole region of Antarctica. In so doing, humans never became specialized to the extent of being locked into a narrow econiche. They retained the adaptive elasticity needed to meet changes in their home environment as well as to move on to new environmental domains, always carrying with them the intelligence and culture needed to face new challenges. Unfortunately, it now might be argued that most of us have become so conveniently dependent upon the artificial environment of our culture that if something cataclysmic diminished or destroyed it, we might be unable to make a re-adaptation to the natural environment, or at least find it extremely difficult.

And so it has been this multi-dimensional quality of intelligence that over the years has separated humanity from the other living creatures. It is responsible for the creation of the life-supporting and spirit-enhancing culture found in the arts, science, and technology upon which we humans are now so reliant. From an evolutionary perspective, intelligence can best be viewed as an adaptive attribute that has enabled H. sapiens to move beyond the automated behavior determined by instinct. It has enabled humanity to coordinate its behavior with the many changing conditions and challenges encountered during widespread migrations as they moved from Africa to populate the globe. The human intellect now has a capacity to integrate various sensory inputs from the environment, to process and store vast amounts of information, and to modify behavior in accord with learning. Human intelligence stands in stunning contrast to the primitive behavior of instinct-controlled creatures. The received conclusion is that increases in brain mass and its accompanying rise in neuronal complexity, and hence intelligence, have enabled these behavioral and cognitive enhancements.

How and why has intelligence grown to its current levels in humans? Many factors are involved. One that may overarch the development of both specialized and generalized intelligence can be explored with respect to the availability of food supplies. It can be expressed in the following simple equations:

abundant food supplies = a lower level of intelligence

scarcity of food supplies = higher intelligence

This scenario goes back to the old saying that crisis presents opportunity, which can be slightly modified to read:

crisis + coping = adaptation + new intelligence

When early hominids began to come down from the trees and gradually transition from an arboreal to a terrestrial lifestyle, monkeys and apes remained behind in the lush rainforests where summertime prevailed year-round and the living was easy. Fruits and nuts were at hand for the plucking. Life above ground in the sheltering canopy of the dense rain forest provided a safe haven from most predators. No new challenges and no new coping strategies needed to be devised. The terrestrials, on the other hand, assumed many new challenges on the ground, requiring not only physical changes but the invention of successful coping strategies. The upshot was adaptation or extinction; those able to adapt were the more intelligent.

In broad historical retrospect, the outline of our ancestral development is not that complicated. About seven million years ago, a primitive group of hominoids divided. Two branches led to chimpanzees and gorillas; the third evolved into our earliest ancestors. Thence began the most prolific growth of any organ in the evolutionary history of life on this planet. By about three-hundred thousand years ago with the appearance of H. sapiens, the size of the brain had nearly quadrupled. Meanwhile, brain size in other primate groups remained virtually unchanged.

The sharp divergence in lifestyle and the attending demands it placed on our early ancestors required a new level of coping intelligence and initiated the immensely important consequence of brain growth[iv]. Those species that remained tree dwellers in the comfort of their homeland, where new challenges were absent and innovative survival techniques were not needed, are the monkeys and apes of today. Survival for them was possible without severe requirements to evolve new brain structures and additional intelligence. Quite the contrary situation existed for the Australopithecines after their move from the trees to terrestrial life and this was particularly the case for H. erectus when they moved out of Africa and into vastly unfamiliar lands. Acquiring scarce supplies of food, devising shelter and protection in radically new environments required mobility, memory and ingenuity. Novel environmental demands for those who would survive elicited improvement in the species, both physical and mental. Stature became more upright and cognitive processing abilities expanded to unprecedented levels. For eons to come, the adventurous populations of H. erectus were compelled to reach for numerous mind-expanding solutions to meet their survival challenges As time passed, this constant coping with changing environmental conditions challenged the need for more complexity in the brain.

---

iv   More will be said later about the role of chaos and the natural laws that have abetted and guided the formation of complexity in neuronal matter.

UP THE INTELLIGENCE LADDER

Although intelligence is not as resistive to scientific investigation as is the elusive nature of consciousness, its measurement has long been a source of contention in psychology. Even stronger controversy surfaces when attempts are made to apply the results of intelligence testing to education, business, or society at large. Nevertheless, amongst the professionals engaged in the study of intelligence, there is general agreement that there is no better predictor of academic success than the combination of past performance (school grades) coupled with intelligence test scores. Recent studies also indicate that intelligence is an important player in making the critical decisions needed to conduct a successful life. And in the general population, there seems to be broad agreement that people who are seen to be successful, smart, perceptive or innovative are thought of as being intelligent.

So now to gain further insight on the nature of intelligence, we will venture beyond traditional explanations of how intelligence is acquired and ask if there is a broader perspective from which to view the trans-species journey that the evolution of intelligence has followed over the millennia. Just as the early tenets of evolutionary biology given by Darwin (natural selection by the environment of those traits most favorable to survival) have been expanded to include new concepts (chaotic energy forces that drive increases in complexity) now new venues of possibilities present themselves to explain the growth of intelligence.

We can go back several billion years and look at how intelligence in its most rudimentary form came into existence. In life's early beginnings, primitive intelligence was quite unlike the cognitive ability we see in humans today. It consisted merely of a rote reaction or two. When a particular stimulus (danger, food) appeared in the environment, there was an automatic response (fight, flee, seek).

As mental challenges were met within and across species, intelligence slowly joined instinct without ever fully replacing it. Behavioral choices expanded in number and variety beyond instinct's stereotyped reflexes that are performed without benefit of forethought. We see a developmental path illuminated by increasing freedom of action and expanded mental awareness. Brain structures gradually became more complex and intelligence slowly incremented to include the multifaceted repertoire of modern humans. These mental enhancements were aided and abetted by increases in brain size as creatures advanced across the phylogenetic scale. It was, however, not a process of total replacement of instinct by the higher brain functions of intelligence. Instinct lingers on in humans today, not merely waiting in the wings to swing into action in times of crisis or danger but also by influencing our lives much as the genetic component of our nature influences our behavior with innate predispositions. So, we must recognize that even today vestigial instincts and drives have influence on human behavior and thinking. Instincts are in our genes. They are wired into our hormonal and neuronal structures. Even though behavior and thought are mediated to a large extent by learning and intelligence, there remains in us an undeniable instinctual component.

We have a tendency to think that animals have instincts and we, as humans, have intelligence. In neither instance is it an all-of-one and none-of-the-other condition. We are not born with a blank slate upon which our experiences etch out the sum total of character and personality. We come into the world with the genetic endowment of a certain amount of hard-wiring in the brain and central nervous system that gives each individual personality an innate content and predisposition. Character and personality develop through the ongoing interaction of hereditary components with learning experiences in the outside environment. There is a mysterious but abiding relationship (yet to be fully defined) in the mix of inherited behavioral proclivities, experiences, and intelligence. This mixture of psychological components colors our thought processes and influences the formation of a behavioral style and learned habits.

One thing is clear. The addition of intelligence to the species has accommodated the learning of new behaviors and provided wider intellectual choices. In a simple environment, instinct was sufficient for survival. But as the complexities of life compounded, novel interactions were required in a changing physical and social environment. Slowly, over many millennia, creatures gained in size and complexity. Bodies and brains became larger and more efficiently organized. Along with this trend, intelligence joined with instinct. Together, they collaborated in a working relationship that empowered flexibility and provided a new lease on life. A newfound cleverness in selecting from an enlarged repertoire of ideas and behavioral options became paramount in the competition for scarce resources and for adapting to the physical and social changes of the surrounding environment.

Thus, over the course of time, the importance of intelligence to the survival of the various species was marked by an increasing role in providing an array of choices. Flexibility of response enabled better adaptation to changing external events. More intelligence meant more adaptability and the more generalized that intelligence, the greater was its utility for long-term survival. Specialized intelligence afforded proficiency in exploiting a narrow segment of a particular environment. A more generalized form of intelligence supplied the wherewithal to take advantage of a wider range of resources and relationships. To wit, as mentioned earlier, when a cataclysmic event wiped out much of the earth's green vegetation, dinosaurs became extinct due to their narrow adaptation.

The generalized intelligence of mammals continued to evolve until it reached its contemporary peak in H. sapiens. Wide-ranging skillfulness in adapting to many environmental variations enabled this adventuresome species to expand into every continent on the planet. And so now we humans use the intelligence that has accrued to us over the ages to study the natural phenomenon of intelligence itself, its beginnings and how it evolved across the many species. Of course, we have placed ourselves atop the animal kingdom as the noble possessors of the greatest amount of generalized intelligence. And, if the convoluted complexity of the human brain is any indication of mental ability, we are indeed richly endowed. When cognitive abilities are viewed in the broadest sense of what constitutes generalized intelligence, we are well gifted and should recognize the responsibilities coming with this gift.

It is not mere brain size that has given humanity the gift of intelligence. In H. sapiens, the brain has evolved greater size and complexity in those areas critical to higher levels of intelligence. This is the case with the cerebral cortex, that new outer layer of neuron-rich brain matter surrounding the older parts of the brain. And it is particularly true for the greatly enlarged prefrontal lobes. It is in these cerebral additions where the higher functions of rational, abstract, and imaginative thinking is done. The older parts of the brain come with their structures in a more complete and predetermined, or hard-wired, form. The more recent addition of the cerebral cortex, where much of human intelligence abides, comes in a more open format awaiting further development by the owner/operator. By creating millions of new connective pathways between neurons, learning experiences provide the potential for additional wiring in the cerebral cortex where billions of brain cells possess possibilities for thousands of connections to other cells.

In a nutshell, we start with an inherited brain structure built by our particular set of genes. This structure, particularly the outer cortex, is then enhanced by the creation of networking between the brain cells to record our learning experiences. The most frequently used pathways are the ones most easily activated for future use. These new neuronal links are the physical analogue of learning. Lack of use can cause certain paths to fade away. In building neural networks, there is a sort of Darwinian survival mechanism at work. Natural selection within the environment of the brain provides connective paths between neurons that are most adaptive. Connections that provide rewards and other successful results will be preserved and survive. Those that do not match the requirements for success in the larger world will be out-competed and wither away. So what we have is an evolutionary competition via the Darwinian natural selection of connections between neurons. In this process, as in the evolutionary process at-large, there seems to be a bias favoring the development of organizational complexity, thus enabling the higher cognitive functions to develop and thrive.

This lack of predetermined structure in much of the human brain provides an openness in the lives of humans that allows a large degree of free will in the creation of individual destiny. If the genetic code were to provide a complete blueprint detailing how a brain is to be constructed and wired, there would be no room for personal choice in learning. Thought and behavior would be genetically determined and we would be robotic slaves to our genes.

As neuronal wiring proceeds during the course of an individual's life, once again we see the unremitting and universal drive to increase complexity. This bias of evolutionary movement toward the creation of order and organization has resulted in a human brain with an astounding one-hundred billion neurons each with tens of thousands of network connections. Such intricacy makes the human brain by far the most highly evolved and complex entity of which we are aware. Evolution has made us the possessors of an incredible cognitive tool. And as evolution proceeds there will be more to come.

John Dervin

DEFINING HUMAN INTELLIGENCE

As displayed in human beings, intelligence presents a multidimensional faculty ranging from reasoning ability to the manipulation of symbols, from the mental processing of sensory data to adapting to internal and external conditions, from the storage of memory data to solving complex problems, from musical and mathematical skills to athletic and kinesthetic prowess, and even more. Some psychologists have identified as many as 120 sub-categories of intelligence. Intelligence does its work by looking at information that is garnered through the five senses and stored in memory as experience and knowledge. It encompasses an ability to grasp new information and act in accord with it and past experience. It is a faculty for comprehending novel ideas and thinking abstractly. Intelligence includes cognitive speed in comprehension and an ability to use verbal, numerical, and symbolic material. It includes the skills needed to do convergent and divergent thinking. Convergent thinking requires rationality and logic; divergent thought employs imagination and creativity. The freewheeling nature of divergent thinking produces original ideas and new alternatives. Convergent mental powers then use logic and experience to narrow down and select the most advantageous of the novel concepts from divergent thought.

Controversy will always follow the footsteps of topics where full and clear information is lacking. The relative importance of the roles played by nature and nurture in the development of life and the formation of a human being is a prime example. The question of how intelligence originates is a perfect arena for the proponents of nature (heredity) and nurture (environment) to lay out their data and argue for the relative superiority of their chosen positions. The competition between these adversaries to achieve eminence for their respective assessments was recently ignited by the publication of Herrnstein and Murray's book on intelligence, *The Bell Curve*. It appeared to many of those on the environmental side of the argument, mainly the press and parts of academia, that the authors emphasized certain data, or slanted their interpretation of it, to favor the importance of nature over nurture. The ensuing intellectual and emotional eruptions were characterized by sharply uncharacteristic verbal attacks, counterattacks and even name calling in both the lay press and peer reviews. One of the criticisms was the contention that the book's hereditarian slant toward the inheritance of intelligence smacks of social Darwinism. This term has come to be seen as implying an evolutionary bias toward a biological basis for determining human differences. Hence, adhering to a strong hereditary emphasis in the formation of intelligence means that it is mostly genetically based and largely unchangeable. This, of course, calls into question the effectiveness of the environment and social interventions. Even more controversial has been the practice of assigning IQ numbers that rank individuals on an intellectual scale. Some see this as pigeon-holing, stifling to motivation, and politically incorrect.

Probably the most inflammable aspect of the book centers around the assignment of collective IQ's to ethnic groups. It violates today's PC code but data should be refuted rather than denied. The statistics presented by

Herrnstein and Murray rank Asians and Jews slightly higher than Whites who are situated well above Hispanics and Blacks. This ethnic structuring by intelligence, combined with the guesstimate by the authors that as much as 80 per cent of intelligence could be genetically determined, has led to the pessimistic assumption by some that the authors were locking ethnic groups for life into fixed intellectual positions determined at birth.

If you are willing to accept the authors' stated intentions, nothing could be farther from the truth. Their claim is that in order to deal effectively with its social implications, society-at-large should be informed and willing to accept certain realities that the scientific community has been aware of for some time. It is their contention that because of its overwhelming emphasis on the manipulation of information and ideas in an information age such as we have now entered, intelligence plays a major role in determining personal and economic success. The influence of intelligence in our society has resulted in the emergence of a prosperous "cognitive elite" who live and work isolated from an underclass. According to the authors, intelligence drives this socio-economic separation. The statistical data they present indicates a negative correlation between intelligence and the social pathologies of crime, poverty, family dysfunction, school dropouts, unemployment, and welfare dependency.

Herrnstein and Murray propose the rationale that if corrective measures are to be found and formulated, the fashionable denial of the relationship between low intelligence and many of society's problems cannot be kept under the table. Oddly though, in another part of the book while talking about the uneven distribution of intellectual abilities, they state that government policies can do little to change the fact of this unequal endowment. Striped to the bare bones, The Bell Curve tells us that ethnicity, sex, and social status do not drive the class divisions in the country nearly so much as does IQ. The vast majority of Americans are grouped in the middle of the bell curve around an IQ of 100. On the curve's far right extremity, resides a cognitive elite with their IQ's of 120 and above. On the far opposite side of the bell curve center dwells an underclass with IQ's below 80.

The authors are careful to offer an admonition against using their data to support ethnic prejudice. They point out there are members of all ethnic groups distributed under the bell curve at both the highest and lowest IQ levels. Even though at the present time, members of some ethnic groups are concentrated in the lower IQ levels, it is impossible to attribute this uneven distribution to the consequence of heredity more so than to prior or existing environmental conditions. In any case, there are many human variables in addition to intelligence that define the whole person. This one human attribute should never stand alone in defining human worth to the exclusion of other variables such as character, motivation, and creativity. We know that personality traits vary in their amount and quality from individual to individual. Humans do differ. Hence, there is no basis for singling out any one human attribute and citing differences in that attribute to imply superiority or inferiority.

In addressing the fever-pitch of the emotion-charged reactions to *The Bell Curve,* Frank Miele, a contributing editor of *Skeptic* stated that, *"Commentators from the (political) left, right, and middle have taken their best shots."* He goes on to say that a group of leading researchers in the field of human intelligence produced a statement in which they concurred with the following conclusions of *The Bell Curve:*

- Intelligence is a general mental capability that enables reasoning, planning, solving problems, abstract thought, comprehending complex concepts, and profiting from experience.

- Intelligence is accurately measured by intelligence tests but these tests are not intended to assess other human qualities like creativity and character.

- Intelligence tests predict future scholastic performance with equal accuracy for all English-speaking Americans, regardless of race or social class.

- As life becomes more complex (novel, ambiguous, unpredictable) the advantage of a higher IQ increases.

- Differences in social environment and genetic inheritance each contribute to differences in levels of IQ. These levels are not fixed, however, intelligence does tend to stabilize during the maturation process and generally change little thereafter.

Steven Jay Gould, perhaps the most distinguished member of the opposition, alleged that if any one of the following four points he attributes to *The Bell Curve* is false, then the entire thesis of the book fails.

- Intelligence is assessed by a single number
- Results of IQ tests rank-order people
- Intelligence is genetically based
- Intelligence is immutable

In response, co-author Murray claims all four of Gould's points are misinterpretations of the book's data and its conclusions, as well as the intentions of the authors.

The American Psychological Association joined the controversy when it established a special task force on its Board of Scientific Affairs to investigate the scientific validity of *The Bell Curve*. The APA offered little new by way of a resolution of this old and tenacious heredity-versus-environment dispute, preferring instead to remain on neutral ground with statements like:

- In short, no adequate explanation of the differential between the average IQs of Blacks and Whites is presently available.
- Several culturally based explanations of the Black/White IQ differential have been proposed; some are plausible, but so far none has been conclusively supported.
- There is even less empirical support for a genetic interpretation of variations in intelligence.
- Because ethnic differences in intelligence reflect complex patterns, no overall generalization about these differences is appropriate.

- In a field where so many issues are unresolved and so many questions remain, the confident tone that has characterized most of the debate on this topic is clearly out of place. The study of intelligence does not need political assertions and recriminations.
- In this contentious arena, our most useful role may be to remind readers that many of the critical questions about intelligence are still unanswered.

It can be conceded that modern IQ tests measure many of the mental skills that are predictive of and important to success in school and in an information-based society. Based on results of tests developed for this purpose, it is not surprising that human diversity and the spread across socio-economic levels reflect real differences. For some it is an easy jump to conclude that these differences are genetically based. However, when consideration is accorded to the vicissitudes of long and separate group evolutionary histories, for example, between European Americans and African Americans, it also becomes easy to see that different environmental and cultural demands interacting with genetic selection have played a major role in confounding the nature-versus-.nurture question with respect to their roles of relative importance. If current-day social and nutritional variations can impact the intellectual development of individuals, how much more so might be the effects of radically different environmental and cultural conditions when they are experienced by groups for thousands of years.

Those early wanderers who left the relative warmth and abundance of Africa and ventured out, eventually reaching all of Europe, were confronted with radically new challenges. No longer would the old, long-engrained ways of living on the savannah suffice. There were new challenges for intelligence and imagination to meet the task of designing the lifestyle needed to find food and shelter and to create the tool technology indispensable for dealing with a strange and sometimes severe environment. Those groups whose individuals possessed a cleverness of mind survived and became the participants in the new evolutionary quest for brain development. It emphasized intelligence and the creation of an adaptive culture that could be passed on to the next generation. During the course of this process, the evolutionary train switched from a developmental track that designed better bodies to one with an emphasis on brain and cognitive improvements. True to Darwinian form, it was the natural environment that shaped the ever-so-slow biological changes in human beings and now it is largely the particular cultural environment that is influencing the development of intelligence.

Intelligence is a powerful and liberating attribute for humanity but there lingers the consternating and unsettled question about its source. Does this profound phenomenon result exclusively from the internal processing of sensory inputs by the brain? Is the brain an isolated, stand-alone unit? Or do we have access to an existing high-level of intelligence from the matrix fields of the universe? This question will be visited later.

HEREDITY VS. ENVIRONMENT

The heredity-versus-environment debate is one contest that has grown long-in-the-tooth during its quest to identify the more significant source of human traits. This is particularly true with respect to intelligence. Critics of *The Bell Curve* for the most part tend to be strong-minded environmentalists. They emphasize the malleability of intelligence and the power of social conditions to nourish or retard its development. Supporters, on the other hand, seem to be mainly psychometricians and hereditarians who emphasize a strong bio-genetic influence in determining human intelligence.

Perhaps as a final attempt to show the extent of the division in this controversy and how it can divide dedicated professionals, we should take a summary look at the work of two researchers, each seeking truth, and each arriving at contrasting views on the origins and development of human intelligence. In so doing, it is interesting to speculate on why reality-seeking researchers following scientific protocols can gather data on an undecided issue and arrive at such polarized conclusions.

ANNE ANASTASI

Anne Anastasi's career was centered on the study of human differences in the development of psychological traits and their measurement. She stressed the importance of favorable social and cultural experience in the positive development of intelligence and opposed a strong influence by factors of heredity. While her studies involved the consequences of the interplay between environmental factors and biological endowment, she remained adamant in arguing for the dominant role of human experience over genetic inheritance. She viewed intelligence as a trait primarily nourished by cultural and experiential factors. She conceded a lesser influence to the *interaction* of nurture and nature, neither of which can act independently of the other.

Much of her research and writings focused on gathering data to measure human attributes and how they differed in quantity and quality from individual to individual. The construction of tests to measure intelligence became the centerpiece of her work. She concluded that intelligence tests accurately assess the cognitive skills needed for success in school and in a society such as ours. At the same time, she emphasized that intelligence is malleable over time and should never be used to label and pigeon-hole an individual. She stressed that intelligence is merely one of many human attributes. The thrust of her work leaned decidedly toward the importance of cultural experience in determining the level of intelligence during the maturation process. She accorded the environment a dominant position over heredity.

ARTHUR JENSEN

During the 1960's, Jensen did extensive educational research by testing the learning styles and performance of minority school children. His goal was to develop a "culture-free" intelligence test without a language bias that would yield an accurate assessment of cognitive ability. Jensen's tests, which could be administered in any language, yielded results that led him to identify two distinct styles of learning.

- Memory or associational learning. This refers to an ability to acquire information and skills by rote memory or repetition.
- Concept learning. This refers to an ability to process and manipulate ideas and symbols when solving problems. Jensen considered this attribute to be closely related to what is measured by intelligence tests.

After evaluating his research, Jensen acknowledged a strong influence for heredity in the development of intelligence, perhaps as much as 80%. The nature of Jensen's research conclusions led to instant controversy because it unavoidably addressed the taboo topic of ethnic inequalities. This was exacerbated by his emphasis on the importance of heredity in determining intelligence since it left little room for ameliorating perceived inequalities with educational and environmental improvements. In his early work, Jensen states:

"The relationship of the g (generalized) factor to a number of biological variables and its relationship to the size of the white-black differences on various cognitive tests suggests that the average white-black difference in g has a biological component."

Jensen goes on to say that natural selection over time has resulted in different breeding populations exhibiting differences in genetic expressions such as brain size. He contends that such differences have *"behavioral and psychometric correlates."*

As a result of such statements, Jensen received death threats and was labeled a racist. Eventually, he would deny claiming "innate" differences in intelligence across races and that there simply existed insufficient scientific evidence to explain the measured IQ gaps:

> *"The only genuine consensus among well-informed scientists on this topic is that the cause of the difference remains an open question."*

Not unlike political discussions between liberal and conservative true believers, the nurture/nature debate between environmentalists and hereditarians will continue until the data become more definitive. What is conclusive is the interaction between nature and nurture. Each of us is born with his or her particular set of genes. This is nature; our hereditary inheritance. Nurture enters the mix when choices are made in the environmental context and new genes are expressed. This indicates that the genomes of parents partly developed through learning experiences can be passed on to the next generation.

CONSCIOUSNESS

Along with a fuller understanding of how the big bang occurred and how life emerged from inorganic molecules, science's remaining major challenge is the resolution of relativity theory and quantum physics into a single "theory of everything". Somewhat surprisingly, many researchers from the hard sciences now include cognitive psychology in this mix of enigmas yet to be solved. They realize that a clarification of the workings of consciousness ranks as a major hurdle to a full understanding of the universe and its natural phenomena. Their reluctant conclusion is that somehow the mystery of human consciousness must be integrated with physics, chemistry, and biology in order to reach an encompassing theory of everything.

Only recently have we begun to view the universe as a single dynamic whole within which we humans are integral, functioning components. Within the cosmic system, the effects of consciousness are now recognized as an undeniable presence in both the q-world of subatomic particles and the observable world of objects and living entities. We are connected and necessary parts in a universe that is an open, evolving, dynamic system that continues today to function as a process-in-action. What happens in the individual parts of an open system is reflected in some way at the top level of the system. Systems theory emphasizes the connectivity and interrelatedness of every part. The lesson to be learned from the study of systems is that we, as individuals, cannot de-couple ourselves from a natural world that is an integrated and actively operating system. Hence, consciousness counts. Behavior matters. Psychology needs to be integrated with physics, chemistry, and biology. And vice versa. The Theory of Everything awaits a viable theory of consciousness, one that includes cognitive psychology, human beings, and consciousness in the laws of nature.

It has not been possible to explain consciousness using the reductive, analytical techniques of Newtonian physics. Currently, several loosely knit groupings of scientists, each with a particular philosophical leaning, are actively pursuing the elusive phenomenon of consciousness. The more traditional group, consisting of physicists and neurophysiologists, is investigating brain functions by applying conventional, scientific principles. Another less traditional group is exploring the newer research fields of chaos theory and self-organizing systems and applying these insights toward understanding the nature of consciousness. Beyond these two groups, there is yet another band of unfettered thinkers who profess that consciousness cannot emerge solely from the activities of brain matter. They contend there is a nonmaterial energy force or intelligence in the world beyond matter. According to this approach, matter (our brain) and non-matter (our consciousness) interact only after matter becomes sufficiently organized to enable it to tune in and process the phenomenon of a universal consciousness. While certain similarities to vitalism exist, this understanding of the world adopts a more scientific approach. It postulates the existence of a universe with an evolved infrastructure that provides a substrate of intelligence that guides matter in creating increasingly complex formations. It does not postulate a divine entity that intervenes in the conduct of natural law and so tends to be more deistic rather theistic, where evolutionary tinkering is acknowledged. The intelligence emanating from this infrastructure, or matrix of energy, is the consequence of the unfolding of natural laws taking effect with the origin of the universe. The rules of operation for the cosmic system were so designed that matter would organize itself in the direction of complexity.

Hence, we are beginning to see how our perception of the natural reality of the universe is determined not only by the contemporary worldview presented by science, literature, and philosophy but also by the interpretive influence of personal consciousness. We often see it quoted that we use only ten per cent of the brain's operational capacity but neurophysiologists tell us the brain is much more fully activated. The important question is how much of this activity in the brain is available to conscious awareness. Neuroscience has determined that the human brain continuously processes several billion bits of data each second. From this huge mass of flowing information, only 2,000 data bits each second make it into our stream of awareness. This means we are conscious of about .00005% of what is going on in the brain at any given moment. In other words, there is a large bank of data about the world and ourselves awaiting the expansion of conscious awareness.

To begin to understand consciousness, we can look at the relationship between matter and mind, or in other words, between the physical universe and our apprehension of it through the spyglass of our sensory brain. One way to begin is by jumping into the middle of a controversy that has divided scientists and philosophers for hundreds of years. Here are some of the unanswered questions permeating and perpetuating this puzzle:

- Is there one world (matter only) or are there two distinct worlds (matter and mind)?

- Are mind and consciousness emergent qualities that arise solely from the activities of well-organized brain matter?

- Or, can highly organized matter tune into the matrix of intelligent energy in a universal consciousness?

When scientists look into the operation of the brain, they see electrical firings in and around billions of tiny neurons. In a web-like sea of electro-chemical neurotransmitters, information travels along neural networks providing us with awareness and intelligence. For many traditional neuroscientists this means that mind is a byproduct of the complex activity of matter in the brain. They see the brain as a stand-alone material device that produces mind and intelligence solely as a function of neuronal activity. To others, the brain represents highly ordered matter that has become sufficiently complex in its organization to enable access to an energy field of superintelligence. The extent to which an individual brain is capable of tapping into this universal field of intelligence determines the clarity of its achieved intelligence. How the brain creates mind is further defined by the tenets of monists and dualists:

MONISTS

These are mainly strict scientists who see brain activity and the many emotional states of humans as a natural outcome of neuronal and hormonal operations. Mind and consciousness are a form of epiphenomenalism, whereby higher-level outcomes *emerge* from the activity of lower-level components. We know from recent discoveries that there are self-organizing, pattern-forming functions at work in the universe and that these bring increased order and complexity to open systems like the brain. A monist would claim that a material system such as the brain can establish neuronal firing patterns capable of creating its own intelligence and consciousness. If, as science marches on, we can design artificial neural networks that organize themselves sufficiently to create their own versions of consciousness, then there would be reason to believe that our brains are also accomplishing the same feat by working independently from a strictly material base. For monists, matter is primary and it creates the secondary effect of consciousness.

DUALISTS

This unfettered group of free-thinkers includes disciples of Descartes, metaphysicians, and serious researchers who seek answers beyond the reductionist explanations of the Newtonian era. David Bohm, about whom we shall talk in more depth later, might also fit here. This group considers consciousness to be an immaterial quality that pervades the universe, remaining aloof and radically different from the material world. Whatever you wish to call this immaterial source (force field, the matrix, an intelligent energy, Creator); human consciousness in some way becomes viable after brain matter has become sufficiently well organized to access it. Presumably, the closer a brain is organized in accord with the order in the universe's intelligence matrix, the more perceptivity possessed by that brain. This is an interactive approach that denotes a connection between the two worlds of matter and non-matter. Each human brain, a dualist might say, in addition to processing the usual information from its sensing organs, acts as a complexly organized focal node into which a larger energy field supplies information, insight, and a general sense of awareness. As opposed to monists, dualists see mind as primary and matter as a means to an end.

EVOLVED CONSCIOUSNESS

Over vast amounts of time, cellular combinations continued to form living organisms that were more and more complex. In lock-step, both intelligence and consciousness followed these biological developments in complexity. In our personal lives, it is easy to see how consciousness unfurls as our brains become more richly endowed with neuronal connections via the maturation process, experience, and learning. As intelligence and consciousness expand, humans are enabled to better inform, guide, and embellish their lives. Many of the afore mentioned interactionists contend that humanity, earth, and the entire universe are immersed in an all-encompassing field of energy and that our brains access and interpret the intelligence in this field as mind or consciousness. Our brains are seen as tuning into this field in a way somewhat analogous to how a radio or television set tunes into the intelligence encoded in the airwaves broadcast through space from a transmitting tower. If this mysterious wave field of cosmic intelligence actually exists, as Bohm, Sheldrake, and others say, it well may be that in time we will develop instruments sensitive enough for detection. If successful, perhaps these devices will help explain how our brains tap into such an energy field.

For now these are unproven considerations and we can only ponder over such possibilities, and if so inclined, choose between alternatives. In broad perspective, it is likely that some combination of the two alternatives, monism or dualism, is true. That is, brains evolve to a sufficiently high level of neuronal complexity and gain an ability to create consciousness and they also develop an ability to tap into an outside cosmic field of superintelligence. Unfortunately, neither monist nor dualist can offer proof positive for their positions. The monists have failed to show scientifically that the rich images, thoughts, and emotions of human consciousness can independently emerge from the activities of matter. The dualists have failed to identify the interface point where the material brain and an immaterial superconsciousness connect, although new research on the role of the aura and chakras is promising. More on this later.

STAGES

In contrast to the unresolved issue regarding the primacy of mind or matter, there exists substantial evidence for viewing the development of life and consciousness as a complexity step-function that has moved its quality forward. Both matter and mind have exhibited a progression wherein developmental pauses occur as nature seeks to affirm and strengthen its position before moving on to the next stage of development. After functions are integrated along a plateau, nature will move to a higher level of complexity. This is evolution moving in relentless step-like stages. Increasing levels of organization are achieved with each stage as each new stage serves as the platform for further development at a higher level of complexity. The biological world, in broad historical perspective, exhibits clear demarcations as life made transitions from fish to amphibian to reptile to bird and on to mammals. After mammals attained the primate level, there was a continuation of advancements in hominids whereby physical development once again paused periodically at stages, sometimes for millions of years. During this most recent phase of evolution, the developmental stages of Australopithecus, H. habilis, H. erectus, and finally H. sapiens were reached. Even the developing human embryo moves through recognizable stages by repeating earlier evolutionary events. During its development, the human fetus has vestigial gills at one point and a rudimentary tail at another. Hence, the saying that ontogeny recapitulates phylogeny is more than just a catchy phrase. And following birth, we reach maturity by once again moving through identifiable periods of biological growth via the well-known stages of infancy, childhood, adolescence and adulthood.

The stage-like perspective on growth applies equally to mental development as it journeys through psychological stages of advancement right along with the physical correlates of body and brain. Billions of years ago, primitive perceptivity began with rudimentary reflexes. The simplest levels of cellular life could sense beyond the confines of their own edges and gather information in order to move toward light or food. This was the beginning of demands on neuronal systems to develop in order to thrive and survive. By reaching out into the environment for survival information, neurons evolved more and more complex networks. This process of elaboration continued until modern levels of intelligence and mind were achieved. And as sensory efficiency promoted survival in earlier days, now intellectual efficiency promotes success in modern society.

At the personal level, consciousness expands from early beginnings of a faint pre-consciousness in infancy to full-blown adult states of perceptive awareness and in some cases even what is considered enlightenment. At the species level, consciousness has also followed a developmental track as it expanded from an early stage of dim consciousness that was limited to an awareness of the immediate environment. Eventually, it moved on to an individualized consciousness, known in humans as the ego stage. Now, some humans are transcending the grip of ego and attaining an awareness of a higher self that is concerned less with the material and more with the spiritual.

We know there is a relationship between matter and mind because we see a correlation between neuronal activity in the brain and the functions of mind with respect to intelligence and consciousness. By investigating this relationship between brain and mind, between the material and the ethereal, we find a platform to gain a further understanding of intelligence. In an evolutionary sense, both intelligence and consciousness have followed a stepwise series of developmental stages. The fossil record along side of tool artifacts indicate that as the physical aspect of human brains increased in size and organizational complexity, levels of intelligence expanded accordingly. Increases in intelligence and conscious awareness have led to a growing realization of the importance of the world beyond the capsule of our skin. More recently, we have gained the beginnings of an appreciation for the role played by the human aura and certain energy centers in the body that enhance awareness and intelligence. More will be said about the aura in a later section.

SUMMARY

Several centuries ago, the pronouncements of Descartes and the laws of Newton ushered in an era in which the human perception of reality became dominated by physics and materialism. Since that time, the main focus of our attention has been on the physical objects of everyday life and how they could be manipulated or acquired. Because of a mindset for materialism and the overwhelming influence of Darwin's revelations, biological evolution is explained by chemical and physical events. Recently, however, there has been a reawakening of two rather old schools of thought. Western process thinking and Eastern Taoism each speak of a flowing nature to the world and a more fundamental reality that underlies the material perception of the world. Because of their subjectivity, these insights on nature did not find widespread appeal during the period ruled by materialism and Newtonian physics. Recently, science has uncovered the self-regulating, self-organizing, self-enhancing properties of open-ended, chaotic systems and now even hard-nosed scientists are seeing far-reaching implications garnered from another world beyond the material one.

Evolutionary biologists now understand that living organisms are ongoing, open-ended systems that take in energy and grow by using their own internal processes to move past periods of stability when these periods are interspersed with episodes of chaotic fluctuations.

During the chaotic phase of this process, new patterns of organization and complexity can sometimes be captured and in so doing find pathways to growth and self-enhancement. This suggests an expanded view of the evolutionary process whereby new psychological venues for growth appear. Not the least of these possibilities is the development of intelligence. This is an important extension to our understanding of the evolutionary process. The surprising conclusion is that, as open systems, we have the power to self-evolve our intellectual capacity.

We have visited a number of novel concepts that when tied together can bring about a release from the old Newtonian paradigm of materialism and create the basis for constructing a new worldview. The next step is to apply at a personal level these emerging ideas about how the world operates and attempt to move beyond the traditional ways of viewing human intelligence and its development.

To gain a better understanding of the evolutionary history of intelligence and the possibilities for its future trajectory, it is necessary first to further explore an ongoing debate between biologists, anthropologists, psychologists, and neurophysiologists, all of whom are groping for a one-best theory to account for our evolutionary development. Many traditional biologists and other scientists have trouble with any hint of *design* or an *organizing force* at work in the evolution of life because this might indicate some form of intervention or violate their self-imposed ban on the concept of progress. For example, Gould, a neoDarwinist, admits to an increase in complexity between the evolutionary stage of the single-cell amoeba and the many-trillion-celled human being but he resolutely argues against the use of the concept of progress when applied to evolutionary changes in life forms. This is a line of reasoning difficult for many to compute.

Other scientists like Carl Sagan and Robert Ornstein have gained popularity with their writings and echo a similar theme as they cling to a random-chance and material explanation for the development of the universe and its life.

Research psychologist Robert Ornstein states,

> *"Understanding that we are the products of these simple processes working over eons will make some of the mind's moves clear. For the mind, like all else on Earth, evolved, and evolved to adapt to the world."* ... *"Our intelligence may have just been an accidental benefit...it seems to me that we will need to understand that independent forces probably drove much of our evolution, in just such a **primeval accident**."* (my emphasis)

And astronomer Carl Sagan expresses a similar belief,

> *"My fundamental premise about the brain is that its workings - what we sometimes call 'mind' - are a consequence of its anatomy and physiology, and nothing more."*

The essence of Darwin's theory is a developmental process whereby genetic mutations present to the natural environment an opportunity to select those traits that will best equip the bearer for survival. One of the definitive works credited with explaining this principle in the light of modern findings is Richard Dawkins' *The Blind Watchmaker*. The theme of his position is captured when he states,

> *"Natural selection is the blind watchmaker, blind because it does not see ahead, does not plan consequences, has no purpose in view. Yet the living results of natural selection overwhelmingly impress us with the appearance of design as if by a master watchmaker, impress us with the illusion of design and planning."*

In countermanding William Paley's analogy between a watch and a living organism and how each would appear to require a master designer with a plan in mind, Dawkins goes on to state,

> *"Natural selection, the blind, unconscious, automatic process Darwin discovered, and which we now know is the explanation for the existence and apparently purposeful form of all life, has no purpose in mind. It has no mind and no mind's eye. It does not plan for the future. It has no vision, no foresight, no sight at all. If it can be said to play the role of watchmaker in nature, it is the blind watchmaker."*

Darwin himself emphasized his position on this matter in *The Origin of Species,*

"If it could be demonstrated that any complex organ existed which could not possibly have been formed by numerous, successive, slight modifications, my theory would absolutely break down."

Other authors explain how Dawkins has methodically dissected and destroyed all argument for a designer or for any preplanning in the workings of evolution. Still, it is difficult not to wonder if such noted contributors as Dawkins, Gould, Sagan, Leakey, and Ornstein, who see the cosmos and humanity as a consequence of an extremely long series of chance occurrences, have discarded their statistics books. The laws of large numbers and statistical probability militate against a pure chance result for such high-level order and complexity as seen in the human brain and the cosmos at large. When natural environments select from genetic variability to put together living systems, the right number of chance combinations needed to reach such a high level of organized complexity is astronomical. The odds for stringing together by random chance the long chain of events leading to the order seen in the universe and its life surpass any number the human mind can fathom. Pulling a million numbers out of a hopper in perfect sequential order would be statistically easier than "lucking out" by making the astronomically large number of correct molecular combinations needed to create a genetic code for living organisms. Some form of bias built into the evolutionary process itself inclines it favorably toward seeking increases in order and complexity. With a built-in bias that prefers higher levels of organization, you would not have a pure chance process.

Consider the human genotype with the enormous number of genes that contribute to the making of an individual. Each gene has an allele, or alternative form, and in addition there are many recessive, neutral, or unused genes waiting to be recruited by environmental stimulation. Multiply this large number of genes by the great number of living entities that have existed during as many millions of years as you care to go back in the billions of years of evolutionary history and you will see that incalculably large numbers are involved in this process. From this extremely large set of possibilities, nature has opted for increasing biological complexity. If there were not a built-in *system bias* favoring the organization of matter into complex forms, it is more probable that random chance would merely have gone around in circles or back and forth aimlessly. Darwin, Dawkins, and others say the evolutionary process was guided by survival instincts but was it a drive to survive that compelled inanimate atoms and molecules to combine until they became so sufficiently well organized as to create the complexities of the first sentient life? The tiny, sub-atomic dust particles that swirled around the early universe and joined to form stars and galaxies did not have a survival instinct directing their behavior toward superior procreation possibilities with respect to their peers. There is another and quite different force inherent in the process that moves matter toward order and complexity. It was present in the evolutionary process long before the advent of biological evolution and Darwinism.

Gould and Leakey contend that because the evolutionary process is determined by random chance, re-running this process would not yield the same results we see in the world today. Maybe if you were to unwind the evolutionary clock and then rerun it from the beginning, you might indeed find a different-looking gaggle of biological specimen on Earth. Remember, though, that the system of genetic coding, which provided nature with choices for its creatures, started early in the history of life with the creation of RNA, DNA, and other macromolecules. The end-product of this re-run of evolutionary history might not look exactly like you or me but could this be anything but trivial in the march of time toward complexity? The intelligent natural forces and processes that early in cosmic history brought together atoms and molecules to make life must be granted their due. Under roughly similar environmental circumstances, it would be these same processes and forces instilled by natural law at work. With some superficial biological deviations possible, would not living entities with roughly equivalent sensing devices, neurological complexity, and hence intelligence and consciousness emerge? These are the evolutionary developments that count! Where are Gould and Leakey's *different results* from this process unless you place paramount importance on the book's jacket and not its content, on the human face and not human consciousness and intelligence? Re-running the evolutionary process with the same set of natural laws at work would bring about the same approximate result, that is, movement from molecular simplicity to neuronal complexity and ultimately to mind and consciousness.

Dawkins argued that unlike the careful watchmaker, Darwinian evolution could produce living organisms without a plan. However, the plan is so pervasively imbued within the evolutionary process itself that many miss seeing it. The plan is intrinsic to the process; it selects for complexity. Yes, the human watchmaker is an active and observable participant in the design and construction of his product but consider the fact that we humans have created automated, computerized manufacturing processes that, once started, produce results without requiring further human intervention. If we humans are clever and foresightful enough to write computer programs capable of directing automated processes that guide the manufacture of all kinds of goods and products without the need for intervention, then this approach may also be the method used by the Intelligence that created the software plan (natural law) for construction of the universe, its life and intelligence. Surely whatever the intelligence behind the vast evolutionary process that has brought about the cosmos and living systems is at the very least equally as clever and foresightful as human beings. Might not that Intelligence (Creator, Primal Force, Maker, or whatever term you prefer) have set up rules of operation (natural law) to guide the evolutionary process in a manner not needing interventional tinkering? As a matter of fact, some scientists are beginning to recognize that energy fields pervading the entire universe serve as both mathematical and intelligence templates that guide the evolutionary process. The templates act as patterns for matter to follow as it forms increasing complexity, and hence seeks to emulate the superintelligence of the cosmos. Natural law directs the formation of matter just as software controls the operation of computer hardware.

Since the time of Darwin, we have accepted natural selection acting upon mutational variations as the molder of the various forms of life. This was thought to be the sole mechanism responsible for making worms look and act like worms, wolves look and act like wolves, and humans behave and think like civilized beings. But recently, there is recognition of deeper laws working alongside these two Darwinian tenets. There is something that generates new levels of organization within open biological systems. Darwinian natural selection of traits by the environment cannot account for whatever compelled early quarks to organize into atoms or for atoms to compound into very complex molecules. Something deeply buried in the process brought strings of inanimate molecules together to create the intricacies of living cells and the genetic code. This process has resulted in continued complexifications and eventually in the incredible organization of one-hundred-billion neuronal cells in the human brain.

If organisms, mind, and the universe itself are random-chance occurrences, as materialist scientists claim, then we must believe that happenstance also created the natural laws that brought about the many rules of behavior for matter to follow in creating the plethora of organized phenomena we see in the world.

The universe-wide phenomena of time, energy, matter and the four forces (See note at end of chapter.) came into existence at the onset of the big bang. These cosmic laws compelled tiny particles to combine and form the first instances of matter. Subtly working at the deepest foundational (quantum) levels of nature, these inherent rules of operation never cease their drive to seek new levels of organized complexity throughout the universe. An inherent drive to become more complex brings cells together to form living organisms and empowers organisms to form hives, colonies, tribes, and societies. Because of certain rules of operation at work in the universe that are biased toward the formation of complexity, simple things become more complex and reach what we call evolved states. This is the missing ingredient in Darwinism. It starts with subatomic particles and proceeds to neurons and minds. Added to Darwin's principles of natural selection and trait variability, this innate quest by open systems for complexity is the means by which natural systems evolve, whether they are atoms, flora, fauna, or neural networks.

Exasperated by the strange and unpredictable behavior of matter at the micro-level of quantum physics, Einstein uttered, "God does not play dice with the universe." Stephen Hawking, somewhat more comfortable with the chancy outcomes in particle physics, once retorted, "God not only plays dice, He also sometimes throws the dice where they cannot be seen." The more I delve into the universe and its evolutionary nature the more I am inclined to take their positions a step farther and say that not only does God play dice with the evolutionary process but that He uses a loaded pair. Natural law has been fashioned such that it tilts the formation of matter with a built-in bias for creating complexity.

That the quest for more complexity moves in a stepwise fashion can be seen in Gould's proposal of punctuated evolution whereby short interims of increased activity can result in the introduction of a new species at a higher level of order. Sometimes these critical periods of high fluctuation and activity are characterized by extinctions; other times by innovative creation. The evolutionary picture emerging is one in which biological forms slowly adapt and fine-tune themselves in a process mediated by genetic variation and natural selection over very long periods of gradual evolution followed by spurts of chaos.

The three evolutionary principles of natural selection, genetic mutations, and the drive for new formations of complexity via open systems combine to shed further light on the evolutionary process but still leave unanswered some of the big questions. Who or what set up the rules by which this developmental process operates? It seems a stretch to assume that the uniformity found in the rule of natural law throughout the universe just happened out-of-hand. Is it possible that the extremely precise values established in these laws were pre-set to produce bio-complexity, mind, and consciousness? Was there a goal in mind? Stuart Kauffman, a chaos theorist, has said, "Not we the accidental, but we the expected." Strongly opposed to the notion of outside intervention in the operation of natural law claimed by theists, Kauffman has posited the existence within matter of yet-to-be-fully-understood laws of self organization for forming complexity. He sees an endogenous quality within nature that negates any need for a "mysterious" exogenous intervention in the formation of complexity. Siding with a new corps of doubters who see Darwin's tenets of natural selection from biological variations as inadequate to explain biodiversity and the phenomenon of mind, Kauffman claims that the self-organization emerging from chaos and open systems offers the possibility of a new alternative.

In opposition to Kauffman's proposal of an inherent quality in matter capable of making things more complex, William Dembski, an advocate of intelligent design, counters with the existence of an exogenous force guiding the activities of matter.

> *"Our choices are, after all, limited. The order we observe in living systems is either exogenous or endogenous – either it is imposed from without by an intelligent cause or it arises spontaneously from the intrinsic properties of matter."*[v]

Upon closer inspection, a happy resolution might be that both Kauffman and Dembski are right, in so far as each goes in defining the source of complexity in the world. Synthesizing their positions, one can state that the laws of nature are an endogenous source causing matter to organize itself; while these same laws have been designed and imposed by an exogenous force beyond the pale of nature.

There are immense implications coming from the new views of quantum physics, chaos theory, and open systems. No instance of life can ever be viewed as isolated and existing unto itself since every component within a system is interactive in the larger system. No longer can we accept the notion that the properties of individual parts determine behavior at the top level of an open system. When properly organized, components produce a wholly new top-level function that is not seen in any of the individual parts. Top system levels organize <u>and control the</u> activities of the parts. Furthermore,

v From a review of Stuart Kauffman's work presented on the internet by William Dembski.

under the right conditions, the organizational ability of open systems can create new and higher levels of order. Accordingly, molecules exert downward influence on their constituent atoms and organize their behavior into a molecular system that does things no individual atom can do. In short, as evolution progresses there are new emergent properties at each new level of organizational complexity. Smaller systems are organized into larger systems that are then empowered to perform functions more complex than any seen in the smaller systems. Complexity increases as each newly organized entity emerges, whether it is the grouping of atoms to make a molecule or the organization of neurons to make a brain. There has been an unrelenting and progressive march moving along the evolutionary scale. Each new level of development in turn is subsumed by a new system at a still higher level of organization. This is evolution in action. When this inherent impulse for self-organization contained within nature is set in the context of evolving life, living systems are seen to elaborate their development in an interconnected web of increasing order and complexity.

But order does not follow chaos unless there are rules in place that trump entropy. The evolution of complexity has not been a random process governed by chance but one that followed a set of rules. Yes, there is randomness involved but the scales are tilted in the direction of capturing more complexity. When natural law applies with such consistency throughout the universe, the consequences of its rules of operation should not be interpreted as purely chance-determined. A better interpretation of the impetus driving nature's puzzling and unending quest for complexity might well rest on the emerging ideas from newer fields of study like quantum physics and chaos theory. While these subtle organizational abilities come from within the set of operational rules known as natural law, we are left to wonder about the source of these rules.

A more complete explanation of evolution's drive for complexity will likely come from a coalescence of these fields of study with the new ideas coming from dissipative structures, general systems thinking, and cognitive psychology. It is possible that an altogether new way of thinking about the workings of nature will be uncovered and that it will be as radically different from our current view of nature as quantum mechanics is from Newtonian physics.

Only by consistently adhering to a set of rules could material, chemical, and biological systems have achieved the complexities of human intelligence. To understand the full story of the evolution of complexity, it is becoming apparent that we cannot rely solely on Darwin's tenets of random chance genetic variations and natural selection. There are deeper and more fundamental natural processes at work throughout the universe and in our selves. Other natural phenomena have also made a contribution to the development of mind and intelligence. Some of these phenomena, including the role of q-fields and chaotic systems, are yet to be fully unraveled.

With the onset of the big bang, the natural laws governing spacetime moved into action and these rules of operation continue today to guide the development of the universe and the evolution of life. If we are to understand the process of how complexity has marched from primitive instincts to human intelligence, evolving natural processes need to be explored, better understood and incorporated in an interpretation of nature. It is becoming apparent that from tiny neurons to brains and from molecules to mind, there is a built-in impulse in the universe that drives evolution in the direction of organized complexity. As humans, we are the evolutionary results of this cosmic-wide, complexity-seeking process. And as information flow-through systems, we are participants in the ongoing process of evolution.

NOTE: *Throughout the universe there are just four forces that move matter, brief described thusly:*

<u>*The Electromagnetic Force:*</u> *This is the powerfully attractive force between particles of opposite electric charge. Particles of a like charge repel. The attraction of the negatively charged electron for the positively charged proton holds the electron in orbit around the nucleus of an atom. The electromagnetic force is accomplished by the transfer of virtually mass-less particles, called photons, between electrons and protons. Above the atomic level of matter, we experience photons as light.*

<u>*The Strong Force:*</u> *It is this force that holds together the nucleus of the atom. Within the atomic nucleus there are protons and neutrons and within these there are quarks. The strong force holds quarks together within the protons and neutrons as well as holding the protons and neutrons together inside the nucleus.*

<u>*The Weak Force:*</u> *This is the force behind radioactivity whereby there is a spontaneous emission of particles (neutrons, protons) from the nucleus of a radioactive material. The weak force also interacts with the electromagnetic force and*

is responsible for the capture of electrons by a nucleus as well as the ejection of them from their orbits about the nucleus.

<u>Gravity:</u> By far the weakest of the four forces, gravity is the attractive force between physical bodies; the greater the mass of the body, the greater the gravitational attraction. The electromagnetic force is billions of times more powerful than the force of gravity. Yet, there is a gravitational attraction between every atom in our body with every atom in and around the Earth; hence it is this additive force that increases with mass and makes gravity appear to be more powerful than the other forces.

PRELIMINARY CONCEPTS

Having introduced a third principle (chaos theory along with self-organizing open systems) to help in understanding the progressive movement in the evolutionary process, it is now time to move beyond the evolution of biological systems. The recurring theme that will haunt these remaining pages is that a finer-tuned way of looking at nature's quest for complexity is to investigate the phenomenon of *emergence* as it unfurls in accordance with a cosmic-wide matrix of intelligence. A universal system of intelligence is experienced by humans as natural law. It draws out complexity as the universe develops. Evolution did not begin with Darwin's description of selection from favorable mutations in living creatures. It began with the onset of the big bang when primordial dust joined to form hydrogen and helium, continued until inanimate matter transcended the barriers to life, continued through biological development, and persists today, most prominently in the growth of mind and consciousness. It is the evolutionary process viewed in a wider scope. This cosmic process has moved methodically from material evolution (atoms to molecules), organic evolution (cells to organisms), biological evolution (species to species), and spiritual evolution (consciousness to soul).

Conventionally, the process of growth is perceived as emerging outward from an inner source of captured energy. While this may be part of the total picture, bits and pieces of evidence are popping up to suggest that we would do well to consider an outside source of intelligent energy that is used to organize and guide development. Some scientists now agree that a high-level intelligence field saturates the entire fabric of the universe and helps in shaping the growth of matter and mind alike. This intelligence is seen as the essential reality of the universe. Bohm, an early contributor to quantum physics, sees energy materializing into matter as it flows from the subatomic realm of the quantum world into the visible world of our senses. Once again this is modern science substantiating the ancient ideas of metaphysics. The revelations of quantum physics sound much like the very old Eastern notions of a cosmic consciousness that informs and guides human consciousness.

As prelude to a better understanding of the natural order that characterizes the universe, and indeed ourselves, a few far-reaching developments from a number of research fields will be discussed. These concepts are only loosely related to one another but when put together they will assist in comprehending the evolution of intelligence. They provide venues from which to understand the relationship between human intelligence and the cosmic reality within which our intelligence develops and functions. Taken together, these innovating concepts supply the background needed to explore new ways of understanding the development of human intelligence.

The development of intelligence can be viewed from a novel perspective when it is connected with some of the emerging concepts that cast new light on the nature of the universe. In proceeding, we will entertain a number of questions.

- Do we live in a world put together by random chance or is there a pervasive superintelligence in the universe that acts as an organizing force?

- Is there a cosmic-wide field of intelligence guiding the workings of the evolutionary process?

- What compelled early inanimate atoms and molecules to combine and become increasingly complex until sentient life emerged?

- Is matter the primary reality of the universe such that mind emerges from it as an epiphenomenon after the activities of matter have become sufficiently organized?

- Is there a more fundamental nature to the universe which influences matter and organizes mind?

GROWTH BY STAGES

The process of growth by stages presents an evolutionary model of movement that ascends a developmental staircase leading from the simple to the more complex. In an evolutionary context, it has been a stepwise progression that started early in the development of the universe when chaotic dust particles moved toward an orderly state. Increases in the complexity of life moved through the worlds of cells, tiny organisms, and animals. This march of complexity pressed on until the highly-evolved levels of organization found in the human brain were reached.

It seems as though nature pauses in its development of complexity to give a newly-achieved stage of life a moment to catch its breath before proceeding to the next level. After functions at a particular stage are reasonably well integrated along a plateau of status quo, conditions may become chaotic and jump to the next organizational level.

There has been a similar step-function seen in the growth of the human brain. Brain growth in those species preceding H. sapiens did not follow a smooth, upward trajectory in their development. Much like the plateaus of human biological and psychological development where past increases are integrated during pauses and then followed by growth spurts, the early human brain during its unprecedented period of growth also experienced step-functions. It is not coincidental that steps in intelligence relate to these evolutionary spurts in brain growth. A complex feedback loop exists between the evolution of brain size and the evolution of intelligence. The evolution of one effects the other such that when brain mass increases, it accommodates further growth in intelligence. And there are instances noted by anthropologists where events caused by intelligence have accommodated new increases in brain size. Aiello and

Wheeler[vi] point out that the two most expensive metabolic systems in humans are the brain and the digestive organs. If intelligence could invent a means of reducing the energy requirements of the digestive system, then brain size could be increased. This is exactly what happened in several instances when intelligence came up with innovations that allowed better dietary efficiency, thereby enabling a decrease in the size of the digestive organs. When our very early ancestors invented cooperative hunting strategies that opened the new high-energy food source of meat, this reduced the need for a long digestive organ and released metabolic energy for further brain evolution. And much later, maybe 750,000 years ago, when early humans acquired a taste for meat cooked in forest fires, they used their intelligence to gain control over the use of fire and began to prepare cooked food. Aiello and Wheeler see this event as an externalization of the digestive system that further reduced the large digestive systems needed in herbivorous mammals like the great apes. Once again, this freed metabolic energy for use in the brain and illustrates how intelligence and brain size shared a synergistic relationship in evolution.

It well may be that during its colossal growth spurt the proto-human brain somehow caught onto the coat tails of a yet to be fully understood phenomenon. Perhaps the early brain latched onto a self-propelling energy force possessing self-enhancing, autocatalytic capabilities whose rules of operation under certain conditions provide the power to craft extraordinary growth by emulating the complexity matrix in q-fields. More will

vi   Aiello, L. & Wheeler, P. The expensive-tissue hypothesis: the brain and the digestive system in human and primate evolution CURENT ANTHROPOLOGY 36, 199-221 (1996).

be said later about the power of chaotic self-organizing, self-enhancing systems.

This same natural order applies throughout the universe as complexity evolves. Even increases in the development of complexity in inorganic matter will move through evolutionary steps. Increases in complexity follow a gradual step-by-step progression by experimenting in a particular environment until the best path to a more organized arrangement is found. That this growth takes place by stages is undeniable. It can be seen in the periodic growth of crystals as they develop from simple to more intricate designs. It happened in the dramatic passage of molecules from inorganic compounds to living cells and living cells into organisms. It can be observed not only in matter and the biological stages of growth but also is evident in the development of culture through recognizable periods, sometimes designated (perhaps inappropriately) as savagery, barbarism and civilization. And apropos to our investigations, it can also be seen in an expansion of intellectual growth starting with the dim pre-consciousness of infancy and advancing to the more powerful mental states of adult intelligence.

In its essence, then, evolution can be viewed as a series of integrations by which smaller and simpler functional units are brought together to become components of larger and more complex entities. The functional complexity of the smaller unit is transcended by the next larger one. This process continued in an upscale series until tiny atoms and molecules combined sufficiently to evolve into living cells and breathing creatures.

CHANCE VS. INTELLIGENCE

There long has been a divergence between scientific and theological explanations of the world we live in. With the introduction of Darwinism as an explanation for the evolution of life on Earth, this confrontation became more specific and acrimonious. Eventually, it was exemplified in the Scopes "Monkey" Trial where the focus of the disputation narrowed to a combative clash of ideas between Creationism and Darwinism.

In more recent times, a third group has entered the fray. They are known as Intelligent Design (ID) theorists and tend for the most part to be non-atheists, some with a religious agenda and others with a science orientation that acknowledges only a need for an originating Source. A second division within the ID group has appeared recently between those who profess a continuing need for intervention on the part of a Creator to complete the universe (theism) and those ID theorists who see no need for active intervention as the natural processes and laws of nature unfold (deism). Naturalists would fit into this group with the difference being that deists acknowledge the need for an originating Agency whereas a naturalist may or may not.

A theme that will weave its way through these remaining pages is a strong inference that the two major tenets of Darwinism (natural selection from random genetic variations) do not supply sufficient information to explain fully the evolution of such great organizational complexity found in life on Earth. The theory of evolution delivers a foundation for explanation but alone may not suffice. Even granting the accuracy of Richard Dawkins' metaphor of the blind watchmaker, something is required in addition to natural selection by the environment of chance mutations in biological characteristics. Evolution, limited to a strict theory Darwinism, is a process of trial and error whereby favorable traits are selected (trial) from chance mutations (error).

Without the presence of a third factor along with the two tenets of Darwinism, a chance-driven, trial-and-error evolution might well stagnate as some comfortable level. A third component in the evolutionary process is necessary to tilt developments in the direction of increasing organization and complexity. This seems particularly apparent in the very beginning when, prior to animal survival instincts, atoms were compelled to join forces with other atoms in order to form molecules. We see this bias for complexity continuing its influence until the convoluted complexity of a hundred billion neurons functioning in the superbly organized human brain was attained. ID theorists explain all of this as the work of a directing principle that is inherent in natural law and seeks for organizational complexity.

From whence, then, comes this bias toward evolutionary complexity at the more basic levels of atoms and cells? Aristotle once wrote, paraphrased, that if the *art* of ship-building were contained in wood, nature would produce ships. In this simple yet profound observation, he cut cleanly to the crux of the puzzle about which people still argue. Think of Darwin's principles of mutation and selection as having produced the tree that provides the wood. That's nature. Art is the intelligence and skill needed to fashion the wood into a boat.

Two thousand years ago, Aristotle envisioned a universe comprised of two entities: nature and art / substance and intelligence. As the recent stranglehold of materialism over world thought wanes, we are slowly returning to the wisdom of Aristotle by recognizing that a strict materialist interpretation of what is happening in the universe is incomplete. A full explanation requires something beyond random activity in matter. Call that explanation what you may – the Matrix, Energy, Spirit, Intelligence, Natural Law – there seems to be some intangible force throughout the universe putting matter together in a quite intricate manner, and surprisingly one that is intelligible to us.

Henceforth, as we proceed in this exploratory excursion, we will investigate what Aristotle has called *art*. To do this, we start with some basic concepts that will assist in understanding the all-important matrix of intelligent energy that is instilled in the very fabric of the universe. Somehow this high-level intelligence pervading the cosmos reflects upon individualized intelligence. It is best represented in the intelligence of the microcosm we call the human mind. The emulation by our intelligence of this superintelligence explains why, to Einstein's amazement, that the Universe is so comprehensible to the human mind. As above, so below.

THE ANTHROPIC PRINCIPLE

We can ask the question, *Is the universe we behold due to a series of fortuitous events or are we living in a designer world?* Theologians are convinced of the latter alternative (that God created the world for us), while scientists and philosophers are divided in their opinions. A somewhat circular explanation known as the anthropic principle (AP) has emerged in response to our appetite for answers to the many unsolved mysteries of the universe. The AP attempts to relate the existence of human observers to the presence of certain specific characteristics of the universe. It notes that the precise laws of physics enacted at the time of the big bang were instrumental in producing those eventual conditions essential for life. Specifically, the claim is that the values of the four forces and electrical charges in elementary particles of matter were set so precisely that if they were slightly otherwise, life could not have occurred. Hence, philosopher and scientist alike have questioned the very precise *settings* that were *fine-tuned* in tiny particles at the very beginning of space and time. These very accurate values were necessary to provide the narrow set of conditions required for life to come into existence billions of years in the future. Stripped down, the somewhat obscure logic of the AP can be stated in a number of ways.

- The universe must have the certain set of properties that it does, otherwise there would be no one here to observe it.

- Why is the universe the way we observe it? If it were not, no one would be here to ask the question.

- If the universe were not conducive to life, we would not he here to observe its existence and wonder at the improbability of our own existence.

> So we should not be surprised by the fact that we
> are here.

In other words, *if* the properties of the material universe were different, *then* the unfolding of natural events would not have been able to create us in our current form. The theologian is quick to say it was God, not the universe, who created us. But the scientist counters that we are a product of the laws of the universe just as much as are galaxies, stars and atoms. By following the dictates of natural law, early particles from the big bang were able to swirl in dusty gaseous clouds and form the first galaxies. Inside the searing hot cores of stars within these galaxies, the elements necessary to construct our bodies (chiefly carbon and oxygen) were created. Then, when stars exploded in supernovae, these newly created elements were expelled into space and used to form planets. And as we now know, there is not an atom in our bodies that did not come from the elements created in stars and found in the crust of planet Earth. In a very real sense, our bodies are composed of stardust and have risen up from the surface material of Mother Earth

Some say the exactness in the many force values and electrical charges that came with the creation of the universe are too improbable to have been determined by chance. Certain others scientists say the preciseness of these values, so essential to the creation and support of life, make it appear that the whole shebang looks to have been purposely designed prior to launch and then fine-tuned immediately thereafter. The claim is that there are too many preset values of the electrical charges in subatomic particles to be coincidental or chance-determined. Without precise settings in these values, the conditions necessary for life on Earth would never have evolved. Stephen Hawking, while not professing a belief in a personal God, has said,

> *"The odds of a universe like ours emerging out of something like the big bang are enormous. I think there are clearly religious implications whenever you start to discuss the origins of the universe."*

And the astronomer, Fred Hoyle, after doing much research on nuclear reactions in stars and learning of the near impossible conditions needed to produce carbon, declared,

> *"… the laws of nuclear physics have been deliberately designed with regard to the consequences they produce inside stars"* (where the essential-to-life element of carbon is formed). He went on to say the universe looks like a *"put-up job."*

Hoyle states that many of the chemical and physical properties of matter are set in an extremely narrow range in order to produce carbon-based life. He concludes since only these exact values are capable of doing so, those values must have been purposely set.

Though not scientific in the sense that it can be tested and then verified or rejected, the AP is helpful in stimulating thought about the universe, its nature, and our presence as observers and participants in the continuing process of evolution. Only in recent years has the narrow window of opportunity for onset of biological systems been linked so closely to the laws of physics, in particular, the force values and electrical charges. Other settings in atoms would mean the elements which comprise the human body could never have been formed. The question remains whether the order and laws we observe in the universe have come about in an unplanned, fortuitous manner or whether it is the work of an Intelligent Designer? The AP attempts to answer this question by asserting that the universal laws of physics and chemistry were so finely tuned that inevitably they guided evolution in the direction of life.

TELEOLOGY

The systems concept of teleology is closely related to the anthropic principle and the question of whether we live in a pre-designed, intended universe or one that has come about by random chance. Teleology can be thought of as goal-directed action. It implies a process, or series of steps, best understood by their end results rather than by their preceding causes. In subtle contrast with the systems approach, the more philosophical view of teleology sees the sheer elegance and intricate order of the universe as proof, in and of itself, that this is the work of an Intelligent Designer. There is agreement with the contention of Aristotle that not only do events and natural phenomena have prior causes leading to their occurrence but also there exists a purpose or final outcome for which they were intended. For the creationist and many philosophers, the kind of order seen in the universe requires an Intelligence behind the design.

The evolutionary theories of Darwin and Jesuit paleontologist Teilhard deChardin illustrate important differences in their respective speculations on how life has developed. Darwin's theory of a strictly natural selection from physical variations is a process that contrasts with the position of those who would include the involvement of a guiding Intelligence in the design and development of the universe and its life.[vii] Some of those within the intelligent design group embrace no requirement for divine intervention by a higher power that set the original process in action. They envision a universe with laws unfolding as a natural process that needs no further tinkering. So, intelligent design stands in contrast with Darwinism's idea that evolution achieves biological complexity through random chance mutations without foresight or a pre-planned goal. The environment merely selects those features in members of a species that possess the characteristics best suited for survival.

More recent neo-Darwinists have explained that evolution viewed in retrospect appears to be purposeful because certain favorable biological outcomes can be interpreted after the fact as goals but the process is not teleological. Natural selection is a mere filter that allows helpful biological characteristics to pass to future generations but since these characteristics are randomly generated, the presence of purpose or a predetermined goal is an illusion.

On the other side of this disagreement, Teilhard sees a world in which the organized complexity of life came about quite differently. He would probably say that the trial-and-error, random-chance explanations of

vii   It should be pointed out that there are important differences between Intelligent Design and Creationism. Some aspects of the ID position have sprung from scientific and mathematical investigations. Creationism is a faith-based belief.

Darwinists are due to an inadequate understanding of the causal chain of events and their necessary outcomes. Teilhard sees evolution as a process that is designed to lead to an intended goal. Outcomes are not achieved by random chance but by an intentional series of events. The goal of it all, according to Teilhard, has been to increase biological complexity to a level that would allow consciousness to appear and expand to a state of enlightenment. In other words, the world is not accidental or purposeless but rather it is an intelligently planned universe with some goal in mind.

Another viewpoint is situated between Darwin and Teilhard. It deals with how intelligent design in life and the universe might result from an original intelligence instilled and carried out by natural law. Such a process is considered to be a chain of events driven by some type of organizing principle inherent in nature. A random series of events does not qualify as a process.

Unless you are a Creationist, the natural processes of evolution that lead to a sudden appearance of a new species are best described by chaos and general systems theory. Biological systems are natural processes that follow the rules of open systems in that they have the potential to self-organize and can move in the direction of complexity and creativity. While this is a feature not included in traditional Darwinian theory, neither does it imply the requirement for a theistic form of intervention to actively guide development. If one so chooses, as I do, the rules governing complex open systems can be conceived of as having been designed in advance by a deistic Intelligence in such a way that the process unfolds naturally without need for further outside intervention, or a "guiding hand." Indeed, one might argue if we mortals with our finite levels of intelligence can devise processes controlled by pre-designed software to produce assembly-line products without human intervention, then surely the vastly superior Intelligence behind the creation of the universe could design a "software package" in the form of natural law capable of producing complex biological products. Using Teilhard's terminlolgy, there is something contained *within* the material used by the evolutionary process that leads *teleologically* to a pre-determined outcome. It implies a natural imbuement that works in matter to steer it in the direction of greater order and complexity. In other words, there is a self-contained impulse within both matter and mind to self-organize in accordance with natural law. And if you are a deist, it does this without need of outside guidance or corrective intervention.

SELF-ORGANIZING SYSTEMS

Systems theory is a transdisciplinary approach that facilitates studying the self-organizing principles underlying the behavior of natural processes. Since its principles can be applied equally well to phenomena in physics, biology, or psychology, research is yielding new insights not only within each of these fields but also is providing a unifying effect across disciplines.

A *system* is a group of functioning, interacting parts that produce a novel result not seen in the operation of any of the individual parts. Systems exert downward control over their parts by orchestrating their component functions to produce a totally new output at the higher system level. Example: the brain is an information processor, the heart is a hydraulic pump, the liver is a filter and together with the other organs and muscles of the body they combine to produce a new system output in the form of human behavior.

An *open system* is one that takes in energy from outside itself and converts it into an output.

> Example: a tea kettle on a hot stove takes in heat energy and converts it to steam and sound.

A *cybernetic system* is one that senses information from the environment and manages its own behavior by using corrective feedback data to steer the system to a desired goal.

> Example: a heat-seeking missile making in-flight corrections to home-in on a target.

Chaos theory deals with the sensitivity of small variations in the initial conditions of a complex open system that lead to wide variations in its ultimate outcome.

> Example: one popular example is the mythical story of a butterfly flapping its wings in the Orient and a year later a storm occurs in the Atlantic. The point is that a small variation within a complex system can create internal fluctuations that eventuate in major consequences.

Currently, these approaches are combining to yield new information about the remarkable events that occur within open, chaotic systems. A frenzy of high-energy, internal perturbations can sometimes cause such systems to lose their order, fluctuate, and then lock-in at a higher level of order by some not-yet-fully-understood principle of self organization. When such perturbations find order at a more elegant level of form and function, a new system is created. What goes on during intense fluctuations inside a complex system that enables it to create new levels of order and thereby to evolve complexity is not yet fully understood?

Some insights have come from Prigogine and his revolutionary concepts regarding dissipative structures. He has shown that open systems operate "far from equilibrium" as opposed to closed ones that exist in a state of equilibrium. This means that as energy flows into an open system there are increases and decreases in levels of activity. When these fluctuations reach a peak, it is possible that new patterns of order can be captured within the system. Most importantly, there are times when these frenetic activities will lead to stability in a more complex structure. When this happens and internal activities find a new point of balance, self-organization has occurred. In a nutshell, this is how open systems evolve naturally. Self-organizational principles can be applied to biological systems, ecosystems, and neural networks in the human brain.

Chaos theory and the newly emerging ideas from self-organizing systems are beginning to merge with Darwin's principle of natural selection to form an updated view of evolution. To the extent that systems theory substantiates a natural emergence of pattern, order, and complexity in living systems, we may not be the mere accidents of chance that some Darwinian anthropologists and biologists have claimed. It would mean that we are the intentional results of an intelligent process inherent in nature and perhaps mindfully put there. According to Stuart Kauffman, humans are *at home in the universe* and are the pre-planned and designated residents of planet Earth.

The *process* thinking developed years ago by Alfred North Whitehead meshes well with new ideas coming from open systems and chaos theory. Both schools of thought picture world reality not as a collection of independent objects and events, but rather as an ongoing process moving in a definite direction. Translated to psychological terms, it places an emphasis on *becoming* as well as *being*. It assumes an openness with the possibility of a number of outcomes rather than the closed determinism of a Newtonian based reality. Such complex processes can be viewed as a series of ongoing steps capable of achieving new organizational levels. Process thinking tends to introduce notions of teleology into the way the universe and biological systems move toward complexity.

Now, recent findings about the self-organizing capabilities of open chaotic systems are updating and supporting the earlier unsubstantiated ideas of Whitehead's process thinking. They indicate that alongside the more basic laws of physics and biological evolution there are principles of self-organization at work. These principles act as the intelligence that has led to the creation of order and complexity in the universe. According to process theory, intervention is not required after onset of the procedure. This correlates well with both Teilhard's notion of an inherent *within* and with system theory's identification of the innate ability of open systems to self-organize and create. In other words, under the direction of inherent natural laws, the process of evolution is reinterpreted as being directed by a universal intelligence that predisposes it toward constructing complexity.

BOHM'S WORLD

As science advances and we better understand the nature of the cosmic reality we live in, our perception of the self also changes. The view of reality once dominated by the materialism of classical physics is fading. New thoughts are entering our consciousness as space explorations and the mysterious, invisible realm of the q-world combine to reveal startling new perspectives. The material world of reductionism is being replaced by an integrated view of a reality of flowing energy where every thing is connected to every other thing. We are learning that there is more to the world than its visible, physical manifestations and that there may even be realms of reality beyond the pale of science. Mind and consciousness flow from an invisible domain that to date has resisted the efforts of scientific investigation. Still, we must explore and investigate.

One of the scientist/philosophers who has ventured into this uncharted territory and brought together new information from a blending of quantum physics, chaos theory, and holography is David Bohm. He has postulated a new interpretation of how the world works. His view describes two interactive realities of mind and matter, though it is not in full accord with dualism, One of Bohm's realities is the explicate (the visible world known to our senses) and one is the implicate (the invisible world of subatomic particles, space, and energy). Bohm's world differs from pure dualism in that he explains mind and matter as essentially the same entity, both of which flow from the implicate world and are merely different manifestations of a single underlying reality. According to Bohm, this fundamental reality, from which streams all we see materialized in the physical world and all we conceptualize in the mental world, is far from the vacuum we normally ascribe to empty space. Rather, it is an energetic plenum chock-full of activity. Bohm characterizes the world perceived by our senses as a *ripple on a vast sea* of moving, creative energy. This ripple (our manifest reality) unfolds from the power of the implicate, or enfolded, primary world that is a vast infrastructure of intelligence and energy. The unseen, implicate world is mother to both mind and matter.

To accommodate this view, one must relinquish the old notion of building blocks of matter as being the basic constituents of the universe and acknowledge an underlying reality composed of a continuous flow of energy. The world is a process in motion and an undividable whole. Mind and matter are contained within this ever-moving field of energy. Both flow from it and while they are manifested differently, they remain connected and interpenetrating when revealed in the explicate world as, for example, the connection between mind and body. Bohm refers to his new description of reality as an *undivided wholeness in a flowing movement.*

Bohm further equates the entire universe with many of the attributes of a hologram. Each fragment of a holographic plate contains information sufficient to replicate the entire picture. In other words, the entire image is enfolded in each and every tiny part of a broken holographic plate. This plate is roughly analogous to a photographic negative except that when a single region of a conventional negative is developed only that particular region appears. In contrast, when a laser beam is pointed at a tiny region of a hologram, it finds the entire image enfolded in that region. Bohm uses the analogy of holography to explain how all is enfolded in every part of the implicate order of the universe. The limitation of the holographic analogy is that it lacks the continuous flow of electromagnetic energy present throughout the universe. Bohm suggests that this implicate order be taken as the fundamental nature of the universe. It should replace the incomplete mechanistic view of material objects since they are only a secondary reality of something more basic. The physical world known by our senses unfolds from the primary q-world of subatomic energy. The energy and intelligence flowing from the implicate world also explain the unfolding of a stream of consciousness in the mind. The implicate order is in an unending process of enfolding energy and unfolding it into the manifest world. Both matter and consciousness unfold as a consequence of the constant flux and flow of energy from the implicate to the explicate, where they become manifest and perceivable by our senses. Unfortunately, Bohm concedes that at present our understanding of the laws underlying the enfoldment and unfoldment of mind and matter are vague.

THE UNIVERSE AS A HOLOGRAM

By using coherent laser beams to create an interference pattern when cast upon a holographic plate, it is possible to portray a vivid and life-like three-dimensional image of an object. This is amazing technology but even more startling is where scientists are going with the holographic concept. Some are breaking out of the old Newtonian mold and beginning to conceptualize the entire cosmos in holographic terms. Armed with the knowledge that there is nothing *out there* other than waves of energy, neuroscientists like Karl Pribram have proposed the intriguing notion that our brains holographically transform these waves into the three-dimensional images we *see* as the world.

When ordinary light waves reach our physical senses they are converted into new waves and filtered through the visual system before going to the visual cortex in the brain where more wave transformations are performed. In other words, we receive a set of waves, transform them and then interpret the new waves we have created in our brains as the brightly colored and contoured images we *see* in the outside world. Much as interference patterns projected onto a two-dimensional holographic plate are transformed into a three-dimensional image, our brains receive and transform wave patterns from a holographic universe into what we interpret as the physical world.

It is difficult for us to accept the fact that there is nothing in the universe except waves. The physical objects we interpret as solid and colorful are in truth only captured clusters of wave energy. Our visual sense deals only with wave inputs. When objects that feel and

119

appear so solid to our senses are expanded in microscopic detail, they appear first as tiny particles spaced far apart; then under further magnification these particles turn out to be only revolving waves of energy. Their fundamental essence is not matter at all, only wave energy.

Other similarities emerge when comparing the features of holograms with the human brain and the universe at large. Any fragment of a holographic plate will contain all information needed to reproduce the entire image. Likewise, Pribram and others have shown that the human brain has similar properties in that specific memories are not restricted to a particular region of the brain but are distributed globally throughout it. Much to our surprise, it may be that we have been gifted with a holographic brain working inside a holographic universe.

While our representation of the physical world may in some ways appear to be an illusory transformation made by the brain, scientists are quick to point out that we should not deny the material aspect of the world. Rather, we should merely understand that there is a more fundamental reality underlying the visible objects that our brain presents to us. The fundamental reality is a vast sea of wave energy occupying every cubic centimeter of the universe, including what we consider to be empty space. *The essence of the universe, then, is an all-encompassing matrix of energy and information that our evolving brains slowly find ways to access.* Just as at one point in evolutionary history, creatures had developed only rudimentary sensing devices that narrowly tuned into their immediate physical world, so now our brains, in conjunction with the chakras and aura, are in the process of taking the next step and acquiring the organizational complexity needed to intuitively tune into the deeper q-reality and its intelligence.

If we humans are an open system within a larger system, a microcosm within a macrocosm, a hologram within a hologram, then the matrix of superintelligence in the larger system can be accessed by the emerging intelligence of the smaller system. The smaller system (the human brain) seeks to emulate the order and intelligence of the larger system (the cosmos). And just as the whole image is embedded in every region of the holographic plate, the universal system of intelligence is embedded in the human brain. The challenge lies in gaining sufficient cerebral complexity to grant right of entry to the matrix of superintelligence.

When Luke Skywalker viewed the holographic image of Princess Leia in Star Wars, it may have been more than movie metaphor. His ensuing adventure to find the princess models the quest of humans to find the holy grail of answers to the deepest of questions. And when Edgar Allan Poe compared life to a dream within a dream, it may have been accurate poetic intuition.

Many of us are predisposed to ask that *if* our universe started with the big bang, *then* what existed prior to this colossal event. First, realize that time and space began with the big bang and both time and space continue their expansion even now. Since the universe had a beginning and continues to expand, it becomes necessary to acknowledge that the universe is finite. General systems research tells us that if the components of a system have specified dimensions, then the total system also must have definable dimensions. It also says that if the operations of the components of a system can be understood, then the function of the total system may also be determined. A system cannot simultaneously have two separate natures, i.e., finite and infinite or understandable and non-understandable. Since the universe started from a single point and is expanding, it must be finite and have boundaries. And since there are parts of the universe that we have gained an understanding of, then the universe itself must (eventually) be fully intelligible.

Hence, the fact that the universe is bounded leads to curiosity about what lies beyond these boundaries. A bounded system such as the universe cannot be its own initiator; there needs to be an external energy source, or originating cause. We know that with the creation of the universe space began to open and time began to move. We have learned about space and time from our bounded experience inside this universe. This begs the supposition that beyond the boundaries of the universe there may be no space or time as we know them. Moreover, we are further led to the suspicion that our universe has emerged from some reality external to it. Whatever this pre-existing external reality may be, it would be the source that gave birth to our universe.

Since our finite minds are not capable of dealing with the infinite, it may well be that the external world that gave birth to our world is infinite and unintelligible to us. This means that scientists are limited to pondering only what is finite and understandable, namely, our universe and its contents, leaving that reality beyond the universe, at least for now, to theologians and philosophers. Since we speculate that this external reality is the source from which our universe emanated, the world external to ours becomes primary and real while our world would be a secondary consequence. We are the superstructure of a more fundamental infrastructure. A rough analogy is that the portrayal of a movie on the silver screen is a secondary reflection of some more basic reality that created it.

And so we are relegated to leaving the mysterious *Source* beyond our universe to speculation but at the same time as the fortunate recipients of intelligence and imagination we can wonder over and study our world. Einstein said,

> *The most incomprehensible thing about the universe is that it is comprehensible.*

It is quite possible that this is true for the simple reason that our intelligence is gaining its comprehension of the world by simulating the fundamental intelligence put into universe by its Creator. This being the case, it would follow that as our simulation of the superintelligence becomes more perfect, the universe becomes more comprehensible by our human intelligence.

With these thoughts in mind, we can begin to look at some of the structural features of the universe that make it intelligible to us. Quantum physics has shown that the material world perceived by our senses is a secondary result of the sub-atomic world. Our perceived world of physical objects continuously flows from the energy source of the q-world. The manifest world we see and feel is the superstructure created by an invisible world of quantum energy. It is not a stretch to conclude that the external energy source responsible for the singularity that initiated the big bang included some of its own essence within the quantum realm of our universe.

Whatever might be our current concept of this originating source (Creator, First Cause, random chance etc.), one thing we can be sure of – our current ideas about this primary cause are probably wrong. We have seen how wrong early ideas and scientific explanations have been and how often our world paradigm has needed updating. We must admit that even the best scientific minds today have yet to describe with full accuracy the true nature of our universe, much less its preceding cause. New generations have always proved past dogma to be either in error or inadequate. So, it is necessary to concede that the universe we live in is not yet fully understood. This being the case, how much more so is the dimness of our understanding of that reality that lies beyond our reality. Stuck as we are in this perplexing riddle, the one concession we might allow ourselves, given the evolutionary progression of matter and mind, is that perhaps we are moving in the right direction. If the life we now observe is an intelligent unfolding of biological and mental evolution, our intelligence may be a groping and slowly advancing attempt to emulate the intelligence that lies beyond us. It is likely that some of this superintelligence residing in the realm beyond our universe also exists within the intelligent order of the q-world. Continuing increases in brain complexity over evolutionary time favor us in this quest for more understanding and higher intelligence.

Q-FIELDS

To understand the potential of the cosmic matrix and the promise of its influence on human development, including intelligence, another venture into the strange realm of the q-world is needed. The q-reality operates according to a wildly different set of rules from the classical laws of Newtonian physics. To enter the weird world of quantum physics, do not attempt to apply what you have learned in everyday life or from studying classical physics in school. Isaac Newton must be turning in his grave in light of what quantum physics has done to his classical concepts of force and motion when attempts are made to apply them in the subatomic world. As we now know, Newton's laws pertain exclusively to the large and observable objects of everyday life and not to the microworld of quantum mechanics. Newton's laws are easy to understand, they are provable, and they yield predictable results. Even Einstein's theories of relativity and gravity, though not as intuitively obvious as Newton's laws, provide an *aha* experience once a certain level of understanding is attained. But neither Newton nor Einstein dealt with the strange, counterintuitive behavior of matter and energy in the invisible and mysterious world of subatomic particles. It is a realm where uncertainty and indeterminacy reign supreme.

When Niels Bohr and David Bohn walked upon the scientific scene, everyday logic took a well-earned bow and exited the stage. The knack of visualizing the behavior of objects when acted upon by forces was no longer possible. Suddenly, energy did not always behave in ways energy was supposed to behave and matter did not always behave like matter was thought to behave. Both were now seen to have a dual nature. Sometimes particles of matter acted like waves of energy and other times waves of energy acted like tiny particles of matter. The world was turned around. No longer did energy flow in a continuous stream. Light was emitted in tiny discrete packets of energy called quanta. Matter did not occupy discrete locations in space. Particles of matter possessed non-localized properties which meant they could be here and over there at the same time. Perhaps most importantly, the well-defined, predictable results of classical physics were replaced by an open-endedness that permitted only probabilities of predicting any one particular outcome amongst a number of possibilities. Complex chaotic systems would break down and then re-organize by means of an intrinsic ability to create something new.

So once again science has uncovered a new way of viewing the world. The new way does not negate older interpretations so much as it limits them to a particular sphere. The revelations of quantum physics are providing additional insights into the foundational levels that constitute the primary nature of the universe. No longer should we view reality exclusively by the old concepts of classical physics and its laws of mass, force, velocity, and gravity. They were and are helpful as we attempt to understand phenomena like the orbiting of planets, the liftoff of rockets, and how the velocity and mass of a bowling ball transfer force to scatter the pins. Now, a totally different aspect of the universe is being revealed in the strange behavior of energy and matter in the q-world of microscopic particles. A duality in the nature of the q-world allows waves and particles to exchange states. Matter can act as a wave and waves can emit discrete packets of energy, called photons. When viewed under powerful magnification, the atom consists of electrons, protons, and neutrons and these tiny *particles* have even smaller characteristics in the form of quarks, muons, color, charm, and gluons. The behavior of subatomic particles in the q-world is very unlike the behavior of objects in the world we can see. The q-world is ruled by organized chaos and statistical probabilities. Outcomes are indeterminate and open to the vicissitudes of ongoing internal interactions, thus rendering only a range of possible results. This is similar to the characteristic behavior seen in the operation of open systems which can appear to be chaotic but may produce new and higher levels of complexity.

Quantum physics postulates a wholly new concept of world realities in which space is the primary source of a dynamic, flowing process charged with incredible amounts of energy stored in subatomic matter. In David Bohm's q-world, space/time is viewed as a realm of flowing motion and activity. The universe is analogous to a flowing hologram. Order flows into the tangible world from the wave energy in the deeper reality of the q-world. Bohm believes there is order and intelligence contained in the unending flow of energy from the invisible implicate world of the minute to the larger, visible world that is our sensual reality.

The significance of this finding is that all matter contains some level of intelligence as it continuously unfolds from the implicate state into the explicate world perceived by our senses and then enfolds back into the implicate. Bohm supports the growing contention that a *protointelligence* is carried in matter as it flows from the implicate q-world into the manifest world. As energy flows out of the implicate world and matter is formed, it carries an inherent protointelligence that guides the formation of material substances in accordance with the order and intelligence contained in the q-reality. Hence, because matter contains this intelligent potential to self-organize, there is a bias toward the formation of complexity. Atoms join each other to become more complex as molecules. Molecules combine to become ever more complex structures until they reach the stage of living cells and organisms. The human brain is the salient example of how billions of tiny neurons have gained sufficiently organized complexity in their neural networks to form a connection with the *mind* of the q-world. Human intelligence results from, and is organized in accord with, the higher levels of order and intelligence in the primary q-reality. As above, so below. As in the macrocosm, so in the microcosm. As in the Creator, so in the creature. As in the Supermind, so in the human mind, though at present the human mind is but a faint reflection of a higher intelligence.

M-FIELDS

It's a wavy, wavy world. We live our lives in a sea of unobserved waves; the universe is teeming with waves that for the most part are invisible to us. Our prime sources of information are waveforms picked up and interpreted by our physical senses as light, sound, and heat. These sensory inputs then create internal waves that are transmitted to the brain where more wave patterns are created and interpreted by us as images and ideas. Everything we know about ourselves and the world is merely an interpretation of our brain waves.

We are waves and waves are we. If the human body is composed of atoms, and it is, and atoms are composed of particles that reduce in their basic nature to immaterial waves, then at our most fundamental level we are composed of waves of energy. Recall the interchangeable relationship between matter and energy per Einstein's revelation of $E = MC^2$. And Bohm tells us about a reality quite different from the physical laws of Newton where the material world is considered to be the primary reality. Even though our physical senses interpret reality as being material in nature, Bohm and quantum physics have shown the world to be immaterial at its most basic level. This includes our bodies and brains which are essentially waves clustered in a concentrated format. Bohm and other scientists have demonstrated that space is not a vacuum but rather a plenum that forms a pulsing web of energy and information flowing into the physical world and creating atoms, objects, and organisms. As a consequence of the interpenetrating realities of the primary immaterial world and the secondary material world, humans exist as an apparent physical form but in essence we are flowing energy systems that process waves of information.

Slowly inside each human skull, evolution has allowed us to capture a small and representative slice of the universe. The quantum wave fields existing throughout the universe are represented in the microcosm of each human brain. Our brain waves are created by other waves received from this outside world and processed into our personal reality. There was a time in our cultural past when the idea of wave fields having power over matter or carrying information that humans could use would have seemed strange and unreasonable. Even many of Newton's scientific peers rejected his assertion that an unseen gravitational field could have an effect on distant objects. Since that time, other energy and information fields have been discovered and put to use in the quest to understand the universe. We are quite familiar with the band of waves in the electromagnetic spectrum that carry radio and TV signals, though our unaided senses cannot detect them. Our senses are capable of receiving only a narrow segment of the electromagnetic spectrum and we interpret those waves as the light and colors of the world. Waves of many other frequencies are used in science and medical applications such as X-rays, CAT scans, and magnetic resonance imaging.

Field effects were first noticed during the 19th century with the discovery of electrical and magnetic phenomena. These discoveries were followed by the recognition of gravitational and q-fields in physics. Now, in biology, the effects of morphogenetic fields (M-fields) are revealing new insights. When growth and learning experiences in animals and humans occur, new patterns of structure and information become embedded in what scientists are calling the M-field. After a new task has been mastered or an idea conceived, subsequent attempts by other members of the species find resonance with newly established patterns in the M-field. The premise is that repetition of previously performed tasks by others is made easier because resonance is found with a similar frequency pattern now in the M-field.

Recent research is finding support for the role of M-fields in providing information for the complex formations seen in living and nonliving matter. This research is demonstrating that morphic fields guide the design and formation of physical and biological objects by providing a template with which they can resonate. The more similar the resonance (frequency) is with some existing pattern in the M-field, the easier a new formation. Rupert Sheldrake has proposed a number of experiments that tend to verify the power of M-fields in shaping the structure and behavior of everything from crystals to brains. According to Sheldrake living entitics in the process of formation lack sufficient DNA information but this information is supplemented when the DNA cells tune into existing morphic patterns. In many ways, M-fields are similar to electromagnetic fields except that they carry pattern-forming information rather than energy. From quantum physics we know that all matter is captured energy and energy is expressed as waves. $E = MC^2$, that is, energy is equivalent to the mass of matter times the speed of light squared. Matter is merely captured energy waves; hence, all forms of matter have their characteristic wave patterns. For example, the contention is that those waves peculiar to the acorn seed and its future oak tree find resonance with a like frequency in the M-field. This connection guides the path of future development of the acorn into an oak tree.

In effect, M-fields can be thought of as patterns contained in the cosmic matrix that supply not only information to guide development of physical forms but also to serve as memory banks for the sum total of human experience. It has become apparent to many that the human brain is best perceived as a microcosm of the cosmos. Our brains acquire a reflection of universal intelligence by tuning into cosmic fields. A radio can be tuned to a specific frequency in order to receive a certain station. Likewise, circuits in the brain, because of prior learning experiences and their memory, can more easily tune to certain frequencies in the M-field. In other words, brain circuits are tuned by personal experience so that certain embedded neuronal wave patterns resonate better with like frequencies in the M-field. This does not preclude the possibility that frequencies outside personal experience can be received; only that our learning and memories resonate more easily with their own recorded frequencies in the M-field.

Experiments have demonstrated that learning and behavioral accomplishments stored in the M-field can make life easier for the subsequent efforts of others. Referring to the many experiments done with birds and animals, Sheldrake claims that by connecting with patterns stored in the M-field rats taught a behavior in one part of the world enable rats of the same breed elsewhere in the world to quickly learn the same behavior. This is accomplished without a known communication connection. Moreover, according to Sheldrake, the greater the number of rats that learn the new behavior, the easier learning becomes for successive learners. This phenomenon has been demonstrated by numerous observations and experiments with animals and birds.

For example, when new generations of rats learned to find the correct path to a reward with fewer mistakes than their predecessors, researchers were puzzled. Some mistakenly attributed this enhanced learning ability to a genetic transmission of knowledge from generation to generation. Resorting to the old Lamarckian fallacy was later discredited when rats in other parts of the world genetically unrelated to those in the original experiment also strangely demonstrated the same increased speed of learning. This eliminated the genetic transmission explanation.

Further experiments have been done with rats, birds, and humans and results continue to indicate that information and behavior patterns stored in the M-field will facilitate learning. In other words, knowledge is stored and then later shared. New learners profit from the past learning experiences of others. Sheldrake and others explain this phenomenon as an ability to achieve resonance with the appropriate frequencies in the M-field.

When a large flock of birds simultaneously changes direction, it is not because those back in the flock see those at the front change direction and follow. The change in direction is instantaneous. There is not a sufficient time lag for a coordinated chain reaction to take place. A better explanation is the field effect. Likewise, the iron filings on top of a wooden table will assume a new pattern when the field of the invisible magnet beneath the table is moved. In a similar manner, all birds in the flock are part of a field of influence and respond as a unit.

As a side note, soon after Roger Bannister ran the first sub-four-minute mile, a barrier that thwarted athletes for years, numerous other runners around the world began to run the mile in less than four minutes.

Summarizing, once a fresh structural pattern or piece of learning occurs and its pattern becomes established in the M-field, repetition is facilitated when a subsequent similar endeavor finds resonance with the appropriate M-field frequency. The important concept here is that the wave fields surrounding living beings are part of a larger field. When an individual's bio-field resonates with a similar frequency in this larger field a communication link is established. Because of this link, information embedded in the larger field can now influence structure, growth, learning and memory recall in the brain's bio-field. Everything is connected; there is just one field.

THE CREATIVITY QUESTION

The creation of novel forms, new species, and the appearance of original ideas, however, cannot be attributed to M-fields. M-fields merely store patterns and information in order to facilitate subsequent growth and learning in areas that already exist. One of the planet's abiding mysteries is the source of true creativity as seen in:

- Novel pattern formations that occur throughout the universe,

- Sudden appearance (on the evolutionary time scale) of a new animal species,

- The cultural genesis of original thought and invention.

So far, science has yet to put forth a definitive explanation for how these innovative breakthroughs come into existence.

The resonance of physical and biological systems with like sectors in the M-field can be viewed as a component of the evolutionary process since a resonant connection facilitates replication, or near-replication. However, the complete evolutionary package must contain more than this in order to have accomplished what we see in the physical and bio-diversity of today's world. There must be another component in the overall evolutionary process to initiate deviation from the norm and move toward creative change. Granting that resonance makes it easier for the duplication of existing structures and for subsequent generations to learn more rapidly than earlier ones, there remains the question of how physical, biological, and even cosmic novelty is introduced in the evolutionary process.

- In the bio-evolutionary realm, neo-Darwinists use the idea of punctuated equilibrium to explain the sudden appearance of a new species. After a long period of relatively small and insignificant change via the interplay of genetic variation and natural selection, a sudden flurry of change can result in the appearance of a new species.

- In the human realm, the source of true creativity in science and the arts has long been an unresolved mystery. It happens, but how? Bits and pieces of ideas, facts, and patterns are

mixed by cogitation, stirred by imagination, then
suddenly and inexplicably they are gestalted into
something wholly new, like a novel pattern or a
break-through concept.

What remains largely unanswered is the question that if
M-fields supply the blueprints that assist in configuring
objects and life forms, then by what means is innovative
change introduced into the process of evolution? We
know that self-organizing systems can, by their own
internal activities, achieve new levels of organizational
complexity. It may be that M-fields also provide the
organizing templates, or archetypes, that guide self-
organizing systems to novel and more intricate concepts
and configurations. When self-organizing systems, also
known as dissipative structures, reach a chaotic level of
hyperactivity, new levels of structural organization can be
seized. The emergence of novelty in chaotic systems may
be a sign the universe prefers to see creation evolve freely
and without intervention. The creative power of chaotic
systems, by their tendency to disintegrate and re-form
into new and more complex patterns, is the scheme used
to find novel designs. Chaotic systems will fall apart and
may reshape in a novel form. The result is a universe that
is a dynamic and interactive system, constantly emerging
from potential to new actuality.

This is one of the explanations given for the
unrelenting upward spiral of complexity in nature. But
not every flurry of activity within an open system will lead
to a novel result. And not every novel result will survive
the Darwinian test of fitness. Some novel structures and

certain original ideas will fail the test of time and wither away.

The human brain attains successive levels of complexity as individuals mature by moving through a stage-like progression from infancy to childhood, adolescence, and finally adulthood. There is nothing novel about these intraspecies stages of development. However, if at some future point in time, humanity should succeed in moving beyond the current species level of H. sapiens, it would be indicative of a truly innovative evolutionary advance. Of course, this kind of creative advance has occurred many times in the past, most recently about a half-million years ago when Cro-Magnon suddenly advanced to the H. sapiens level. And a few million years prior to that event, H. erectus moved up the evolutionary ladder to become Cro-Magnon.

As species advanced at the biological level, there were attending advances in cultural achievements, fueled by the energy of new ideas and invention. To explain the origin of true novelty in the process of evolution, it is necessary to go beyond Darwin and natural selection and look at the role of q-field effects on the evolutionary process.

We know that living systems have triumphed over the second law of thermodynamics which says that everything in the universe is in a state of increasing disorder, or entropy. However, in opposition to entropy, living systems are self-organizing systems. They are described by Prigogine to have the capability of creating their own order. This new order achieved by living systems is in itself an act of creativity. As a result of the power invested in self-ordering systems, living entities, particularly at the human level, are endowed with an innate drive to organize and create. It started in the physical world when self-organizing systems of atoms and molecules began to compound. The evolutionary process carried the principles of these systems into the bio-physics of living creatures. As long as matter or energy can flow into open systems, their parts can be drawn together and organized into larger, more elaborate systems with features not contained in any of the constituent parts. Hence, the drive to create order in the activities of mind is inborn. As a continuation of the laws of evolution, we are self-organizing systems that seek to create order and complexity. This is done behaviorally as we create our own lives by choosing certain alternatives over others. It is done intellectually when we mix and match concepts in innovative ways.

However, creativity and intelligence are not achieved by brain power alone. We are a composite of elements (body, brain, aura, spirit, etc.) and as such we function as open systems. In turn, each of us is a part in a larger system. As an individual human being, we are a subsystem of a larger cosmic system. In an open system, information is shared; it passes back and forth between system components, which are subject to top-down operational control. This means that human intelligence and creativity need not rely exclusively on an isolated brain. As will be discussed later, the human aura and chakras act as antennae to provide a critical interface between the brain and the information and intelligence contained in the universe's q-fields.

THE AP REVISITED

The Anthropic Principle (AP) seeks to shed light on why we are here as observers of the universe wondering why we are here and why our planet is so bio-friendly. The AP asserts that if certain critical constants were only slightly different, the conditions conducive to life would not exist and we would not be here asking the question, "Why are we here?" Typically, the AP is stated in three forms. (From *The Anthropic Cosmological Principle*, Barrow and Tipler, 1986)

- The Weak AP: There are finely-tuned forces and electrical charges in matter that are so precisely set that the development of life was an inevitable outcome.

- The Strong AP: The universe has those specific properties that enabled life to develop after a certain amount of evolutionary time and enabled the appearance of observers to witness development in the cosmos.

- The Fixed AP: Intelligence and information processing must come into existence in the Universe and, once it comes into existence, it will never die out.

There are further confounding anomalies whose occurrence is difficult to fathom and without whose presence life and intelligence as we know them would not exist. M-theory posits that in addition to time the universe contains ten spatial dimensions. Yet only three of these were expanded when cosmic inflation occurred immediately following the big bang. If some number other than three had expanded, things would be altogether different. In addition to the precise settings for three dimensional space, there were other settings which, if minutely different, would not have led to the development of intelligent life. For example, if the explosive power of the big bang were of a slightly greater magnitude, the primordial particles would have scattered with such velocity that the cosmos would be essentially empty. And if the explosive force were less, the universe would have collapsed in the Big Crunch long before life could evolve. Steven Hawking speaks of this mysterious precision:

> *Why is the universe so close to the dividing line between collapsing again and expanding indefinitely? In order to be as close as we are now, the rate of expansion early on had to be chosen with fantastic accuracy.*

On this same topic, James Gardner points out that:

> *It is not only the rate of cosmic expansion that appears to have been selected with phenomenal precision in order to render our universe fit for carbon-based life and the emergence of intelligence. A multitude of other factors are fine-tuned with fantastic exactitude to a degree that renders the cosmos almost spookily bio-friendly. Some of the universe's life-friendly attributes include the odd proclivity of stellar nucleosynthesis —*

> *the process by which simple elements like hydrogen*
> *and helium are transmuted into heavier elements*
> *in the hearts of giant supernovae – to yield copious*
> *quantities of carbon, the chemical epicenter of life as*
> *we know it.*

Fred Hoyle is a famed astronomer who has done extensive research on nuclear reactions occurring in the core of stars. He claims that in order to achieve the complex string of chemical reactions required for the production of carbon, someone must have *tinkered* with the settings.

Both scientists and theologians find support for their views in the AP while other members in these same two groups discredit the idea as being meaningless and using circular logic. Unfortunately, the AP is too elusive to test scientifically for its truth or nonsense. But the value of the AP may lie in its unanswerable elusiveness. The important questions are those that cannot be answered at the present time.

By way of further explanation, creationists merely say it was God who has established the universe with *preplanned* conditions conducive to supporting life. The scientist retorts that Earth's life-friendly conditions are simply the expected consequences of the natural laws and physical constants at work throughout the Universe. This leads to the inevitable question of whether the cosmos and its life are the results of unplanned consequences or whether there is some form of intelligence at work in the Universe. There are those scientists who subscribe to the view that life is a chance occurrence. Others contend that, given the initial conditions obtaining at the moment of the big bang and the subsequent initiation of natural law, there has been a relentless cosmic and biological evolution moving in the direction of complexity and logically culminating in life, mind, and intelligence.

Those who see the Universe coming about through a long series of chance events tend, for the most part, to be atheists. It is unclear how atheists explain the origin of the natural laws that so consistently govern activity in the Universe but theists and deists see natural law as part of the original package that accompanied creation. Theists and deists do, however, have their fundamental disagreement regarding the role of a Creator in evolution. Theists conceive of an actively involved Creator who participates in the development of the universe and even intervenes (through miracles) in the workings of natural law. Deists see a more reserved Creator who set up the initial conditions of creation, established natural laws, and now sits back to watch the development of a cosmos without intervening.

So what does the AP reveal about intelligence, its source, and its development? It suggests that if there is a cosmic intelligence underlying the development of the incredibly diverse complexity in the universe, then it is not unreasonable to conclude that the evolutionary processes inherent in the universe are the root cause behind the neural complexity. Given that our neural complexity is emulating the structural organization of the universe, we can conclude that our intelligence is emerging from a larger system of cosmic intelligence. Thus, it is not surprising that our brains are instilled with a natural drive to explore human origins.

INTELLIGENCE RISING

INTRODUCTION

First, a word of caution. Although our knowledge of the universe has grown immensely in recent years, it mostly involves that tiny portion of matter that we can actually see. The mysterious presence of dark matter is inferred by the powerful gravitational forces it exerts on visible matter, specifically stars and galaxies. The vast majority of matter in the universe (some say as much as 90%) is dark matter and it is almost a total mystery to scientists.

An important mind-set for scientist and religionist alike is openness to the strong possibility of error in one's current belief system. There is little tenacity difference in the dogmatism of the faith-based beliefs of a creationist and the lifelong commitment of a scientist to his chosen set of theories. Granted that a certain level of commitment is needed to pursue with fervor a particular ideology; however, when commitment reaches a myopic level that closes off new information about alternative possibilities, the resulting condition is counterproductive.

Some scientists as well as religious fundamentalists allow themselves to be caught in this trap. Years ago, Max Planck said, "A new scientific truth does not triumph by convincing its opponents and making them see the light, but rather because its opponents eventually die, and a new generation grows up with it." So we proceed with the realization that science's history has been a succession of new ideas and theories elaborating upon and replacing older ones.

We also must acknowledge, as cited in *What the Bleep Do we Know!?*, that there is immense activity in our brains ceaselessly occurring beneath our level of conscious awareness:

> *Given that we are only aware of 2000 bits of information out of the 400 billion bits of information we are processing per second ... when we argue against new knowledge, how much of our 'awareness' is arguing! How can we know about all the things that we do not know?*

The operation of the human mind has long been an alluring marvel to those who observe it and a perplexing enigma to those who study it. Even today in this advanced age of science, the brain remains largely mysterious when probed beneath the level of its ability to process sensory inputs. And even more elusive and difficult to decipher is how the mind creates consciousness. Enabled by its architectural design, empowered by a high level of neuronal organization, and driven by some unidentified quest to *know*, the human brain/mind system is making a valiant but unfinished attempt to identify and emulate the source of its intelligence.

It is important to understand what is and what is not meant by the term *intelligence* when applied to humans. Often there is a tendency to use the term 'intelligence' in describing the performance of computer-controlled devices. For example, robotic behavior is said to be controlled by artificial intelligence (AI). However, to be intelligent in the sense that humans are intelligent, AI would need to demonstrate a capability not only to adapt to changing external conditions but to evolve to higher levels intellectual capability. This means doing more than selecting on cue certain software programs to guide automatic behavior. To be comparable to human intelligence as it has evolved in H. sapiens, AI would need not merely to choose suitable chunks of software at appropriate times, it would need to continuously test, and rewrite its own software in response to internal and external conditions. The human brain creates and applies ideas using a selective process not unlike biological evolution, except on a much shorter time scale. Brain circuits that provide favorable results are retained while those that are not frequently used fade away. Hence, the term intelligence is reserved for processes that go beyond the manipulation of data by preinstalled instructions. It includes an uncanny ability to respond flexibly to unforeseen circumstances in an ongoing process of adapting and evolving.

AS ABOVE, SO BELOW

In all that follows, it will be necessary to guard against being too dogmatic or overly enamored of current theories on the nature of intelligence and its development. Much is yet to be learned. After all, it was only a century ago that the nature of matter was unknown. Some scientists speculated on the existence of atoms; others rejected the idea of tiny atoms as unproven and unprovable. Today, we not only have an understanding of atoms, once thought to be the indivisible foundation of all matter, but we have uncovered the atom's many tiny constituent parts. Atoms are composed of protons, neutrons and electrons and even further analysis indicates microscopic particles like muons, hadrons, quarks, mesons, and leptons.

What does this have to do with being dogmatic about theories of intelligence? We must realize that we possess only fragments of knowledge about the nature of the universe. The same is true for the human condition. Much remains to be discovered. For example, the physical matter and energy we are familiar with here on Earth and what we can see of it in the other planets, stars, and galaxies constitute only a tiny portion of the material and energy in the universe. (Remember that matter and energy can be converted, one to the other: $E = MC^2$) Scientists tell us that their experiments and observations indicate that we are ignorant of 95% of what makes up the universe. There is five times more dark matter, undetected except for the effects of its presence, in the universe than the kind of matter with which we are familiar. The presence of dark matter is known only by its gravitational effects, and yet together, dark matter and visible matter comprise only 30% of the universe. The surprising conclusion is that the remaining 70% of the universe consists of dark energy. This unseen force is the strange property of *empty* space that accelerates the galaxies at ever-increasing rates of speed as they flee from one another, accounting for the expanding nature of the universe.

At the very least, we are learning the extent of our information deficit since it has become apparent that there are energies and forces at work in the universe about which we know virtually nothing. However, thanks to the revelations of quantum physics, we do know there is incredible order and intelligence contained deep within the fabric of the universe. The suggestion has been made that an intelligence matrix permeates the universe and acts as a template in guiding the physical and mental development of life in accordance with its own design. Rupert Sheldrake has proposed that human learning and behavior are facilitated by information contained in morphogenetic fields. It well may be that human intelligence emulates not only these morphogenetic templates but imitates the structure in the superintelligence contained in the universe's well-ordered q-fields.

The limitations seen in human mental attributes can be interpreted as our still-incomplete attempt to replicate in the design of our bodies and brains the order and intelligence of the universe. The extent of the efficiency with which this emulation can be accomplished is significantly determined at birth by the inherited structures of the brain and by the new networks subsequently developed by learning experiences. A whole and healthy newborn brain has a design with certain innate capabilities for capturing some portion of the order and intelligence contained in the universe. Subsequently, the brain's structural design is augmented by neural connections made during the long process of learning.

So once again, we return to the nature-nurture conundrum. In the past, the question has been about the degree to which each of these two factors plays a role in the determination of intelligence. Now a third player has been added to the mix to further confound the question. It is beginning to appear there is a three-way interaction between nature, nurture, and the human aura. New research indicates the aura has been added to the mix as the three factors seek an emulation of higher forms of intelligence. The new challenge lies in the unveiling of how this three-part interaction results in the development of human intelligence.

As it develops from an interplay of environment, brain, and aura, human intelligence becomes more able to tune into a matrix of cosmic superintelligence. Psychologists should join physicists in studying the nature of the intelligent order in the wave energy emanating from the q-world. David Bohn talks of an implicate reality in the q-world that brings intelligence and order into the explicate world, where the perceived reality of our senses exists. As brain matter slowly organizes in the explicate world, it approximates a closer replication of the order and intelligence emanating from the implicate q-world. The fields of the implicate world make up the fundamental reality from which energy flows into the explicate world. Our perceived world, then, is a secondary effect of a primary q-reality; hence, the world accessible to our senses is an epiphenomenon of something more basic.

This may seem ethereal and unrealistic to the practical mind but remember that until recently science did not accept the notion of waves exerting influence over material objects or even their ability to carry information. The possibility of gravity fields affecting distant objects was viewed with skepticism by most of Newton's peers. We now know that the electromagnetic fields carry not only the well-ordered waves of light available to our senses but also that such waves are capable of carrying intelligence, i.e., radio and television signals.

Scientists have a reasonably good understanding of how the various light waves representing shape and color create for us the experience of a visual scene. The stimulus of light waves from a scene falls upon the retina, activates a micro-electrical signal that moves along the optic nerve and induces the further firing of neurons in the brain's visual cortex. This neuronal activity becomes the internal representations that we holographically interpret as a colorful external scene. But there are only waves entering the brain to reflect the outside world and there are only more waves representing these waves inside the brain. Incoming sensory waves create signals in the brain known as *neuronal correlates*. Scientists have studied the relationship between incoming waves and the resultant firing of neural networks in the brain and they are comfortable with the fact that these neuronal correlates accurately represent the visual and sound waves we *see* and *hear*. Still, we are dealing only with incoming sensory waves that stimulate a new set of waves for the brain's processing. No wonder a 19th century neurophysiologist once said, "All I know are my nerves."

If you are willing to accept the proposition supported by quantum physics of a supremely organized energy field throughout the universe, then there is the further possibility that each human aura connects with this larger field of intelligence. After all, both humans and the universe are products of the same creative process and are integrated in a wholistic system. The brain receives communication from the senses and the aura from a universal field of intelligence. All are engaged in an interactive process of sending and receiving signals. The challenge then is to form brain structures that enable human intelligence to be more in accord with the larger universal field of intelligence.

Thus, humans mirror an incomplete and shadowy reflection of a superintelligence tuned in by the aura and transmitted to the brain via wave signals. The human brain, itself a wave detecting and processing device, would then be the recipient of signals from the physical senses and its surrounding electromagnetic aura. Humans, as integrated parts of an undivided cosmic system, this is a further example of how all components interact in a dynamic manner.

THE AURA

Sometimes known as the human energy field, the aura is a spectrum of energy or light waves surrounding the physical body. Just as the Earth is surrounded by a magnetic field so the human body is surrounded by a field of faint electrical energy. The presence of the aura and its powers are yielding surprising information. Because of its higher frequency, the aura is not readily detectable by the human eye although its presence has been talked about for centuries and has been mentioned in many cultures. In many traditions, the auric halo signifies a saint or a highly evolved adept.

In addition to the aura, there is a great deal *out there* that we cannot see because their energy waves differ in frequency from the narrow range of light waves visible to humans. The frequency range accessible to the human eye accounts for a miniscule $1/100,000^{th}$ of the full range of the electromagnetic energy spectrum. In other words, the visible light we see as colors amounts to a single tick on a scale with 100,000 ticks. Science has shown that in its most fundamental nature the universe consists of waves of quantum energy. Notwithstanding that our senses tell us there is solid matter in the world and that for years the atom was believed to be the fundamental building block of the material universe, we now know there is nothing in the universe but waving fields of energy. Matter is nothing more and nothing less than captured wave energy with large amounts of space between its widely separated atoms.

In a manner not dissimilar to the information contained in radio and television waves sent out from broadcasting towers, intelligence is contained in the organized patterns of wave energy that exist throughout the universe. It is quite possible that human intelligence, via the brain and aura, tunes in this universal intelligence in an attempt to emulate its order. There is accumulating information that both matter and life organize in accord with patterns in a cosmic matrix. It is difficult to ignore that some intelligent force compels atoms to combine and guides their compounding into more complex molecules. The evolutionary process can be looked upon as an inexorable march from simple states of matter to more complex ones, from atoms to cells, from cells to neurons, and from neurons to the most complex grouping of matter known to us, the human brain.

The brain receives only wave inputs from the outside world and transforms these signals by Fourier analysis into the images and ideas of our physical and intellectual lives. The aura comes into play by acting as mediator between the brain and the fields of intelligence contained in the universe. We know that the brain was not designed for us from scratch. Rather, it is a three-part system that was first used by reptiles (the old brain) and then modified with a new addition for use by mammals (the mid-brain). The next brain update occurred when the homo genus received a new layer of brain material wrapped around the older brain. In recent evolutionary times this third add-on, the cerebral cortex (new brain), has enabled the higher cognitive functions of H. sapiens. The next evolutionary step will entail a fourth add-on, probably only after the brain becomes more fully integrated with the aura. This will form a more complex system and enable further tuning in of the wave intelligence in the universal matrix.

Many of the frequencies in the universal energy field are higher than ones that the human brain can handle. This is why the aura in conjunction with the body's seven energy centers (sometimes called energy vortexes or chakras) are needed to transform these higher levels of energy into the lower frequencies usable by the human brain. The aura and chakras can be compared to the transformers seen on power poles. The main power lines carry high voltages which, if not reduced by transformers, would destroy all of the appliances in your house. In like manner, the aura and charkas transform the high frequencies of the universal power web into the lower frequencies amenable to the brain and other organs. With success in expanding mind and awareness and integrating the aura and chakras comes an ability to access this field of high-frequency energy. The aura and the seven chakras are an interface between the physical and the nonphysical, between our brain and the intelligence contained in the q-world.

More and more we should think of ourselves not as a material entity but as a receptive nodal point for waveforms in a universe whose essence is flowing energy. Einstein and quantum physics tell us that matter and energy are interchangeable ($E=MC^2$) and that each is merely a different aspect of a common underlying reality. As we begin to understand ourselves in the context of energy beings we become aware that we are organized in such a way that our brains, in conjunction with its surrounding bioenergy field, can access and decipher the intelligence in a larger universal energy field. It is within a field laden with energy and intelligence that we live. As we achieve greater resonance with the higher frequencies in this field, human intelligence will respond correspondingly. Accessing a higher state of consciousness and intelligence is not unlike tuning in stations at various frequencies on the radio dial. In order to reach the higher frequencies in the quantum matrix, it is necessary to meditatively re-tune the brain via the chakras and aura.

Sensitive electronic instruments are used to measure frequency activity in the heart and brain and this activity can then be shown as a series of waves on a screen. Typically, brain waves will reach about 100 cycles per second (cps) and bio-frequencies of the heart will range up to around 250 cps. Instruments with even greater sensitivity can detect the energy field of the aura surrounding the physical body, where frequencies can reach 1600 cps, and higher.

The strongest signals from the body's energy fields exist around seven energy centers. These seven vortexes begin at the base of the spine and ascend to the crown. Commonly known as chakras, they connect the physical body and brain with the matrix of intelligence in the q-world. Each chakra is linked to one of the seven endocrine glands and together they act as transformers to reduce the higher frequencies of the matrix to levels the human body can utilize. In a sense the chakras are tuned antennae each accepting a certain frequency. The seven chakra frequencies correspond to the wavelengths of the seven primary colors of the visible light spectrum.

One researcher, Valerie Hunt of UCLA, has achieved remarkable results by showing that specific wave patterns on an oscilloscope taken from the surrounding aura correlate with the specific colors that appear in the human aura. The colors in the aura correlate with levels of personal evolvement. Dr. Hunt's research is being done with individuals whose levels of consciousness fall into three categories:

1) Those with typical states of consciousness where the primary focus is on the material aspect of the

world. Frequencies found in the energy fields of such individuals are usually in the vicinity of 250 cps.

2) Those individuals who have displayed an ability to heal others have frequency levels that were shown to range up to 800 cps.

3) And those categorized by Hunt as *mystical personalities* having deep knowledge and wisdom about themselves and the world. These highly evolved people have auric frequencies that virtually go off the chart, some reaching as high as 20,000 cps.

The results of her research indicate that as consciousness is expanded and new levels of intelligence are integrated, the frequencies detected in the human aura increase. This is in keeping with many traditions that talk about highly evolved spiritual people existing on a higher vibrational plane. Dr. Hunt's conclusion is that the energy fields of the aura indicate that mind and intelligence are not limited to the operations of a stand-alone brain. The human aura can access informational frequencies beyond those available to the brain alone. As we learn more about our surrounding field of bioenergy, we can use it as an adjunct to the brain and employ its potential for accessing the intelligence needed to guide thought and behavior.

For the past several centuries, our levels of awareness and intellectual growth have been limited by an obsession with the material nature of the world. Now, science has succeeded in penetrating a little deeper into the true nature of the world and humanity. From a scientific view point, the new bottom-line is that our essential nature is that of frequency beings. Even though the physical body and its brain function at levels below much of that in the cosmic intelligence field, we can learn to access the higher frequency levels. Step by step, we can take advantage of this valuable new resource by developing the skills for gaining access to the aura and its ability to tune into the quantum-wave intelligence pervading the universe. No longer should we view the brain as an isolated system for receiving and processing only sensory information. Rather, each of us is a functioning part of the larger cosmic system of intelligence. This calls into question the scientific imperative held by many scientists that intelligence emerges solely from the biochemical activities of matter in the brain. The modern human being functions as a component in a system that includes an interaction of body, brain, and aura with a connection to a cosmic-wide field of order and energy. The natural order of the universe is contained in the q-world and from this fundamental source intelligence flows into human life.

THE Q-REALITY

There are two schools of thought regarding the phylogenetic path protohumans followed on the long birthing journey that has led to modern humanity. About 2.5 million years ago, many members of H. erectus left Africa in search of a new life. This was done partly because they were an adventurous sort and possibly also because they were the less robust or aggressive members of the species. They may have been forced *out of Africa* by stronger claimants to the land. In either case, the new wanderers were equal to the challenges that confronted them as they moved out of their savanna homeland into the Middle East and eventually throughout much of Europe and Asia.

In time, H. erectus would evolve into H. sapiens but there remains a question as to the actual location where H. sapiens first appeared. Did those members of H. erectus who remained behind evolve into H. sapiens somewhere in eastern Africa? Or, during the migrations of H. erectus after leaving Africa, did H. sapiens evolve in a number of places across the Middle East, Asia, and Europe?

There are many who favor the *Out-of-Africa* theory whereby H. erectus evolved into H. sapiens while still in Africa and then this new, larger-brained breed migrated along the earlier paths of H. erectus, out-competing and replacing them, as well as the Neanderthals, by virtue of superior intelligence and technology. H. sapiens eventually would occupy large portions of the Middle East, Asia, and Europe while many of the species who remained in Africa expanded into distant parts of that continent. After a long time on separate evolutionary paths covering several continents, the demands of different environments resulted in minor variations in certain physical characteristics and mental skills. Those nomadic seekers of a new life who left the mild weather conditions and relative security of their homeland were soon confronted with environmental severities that necessitated a greater dependence upon novel adaptations. Wit and intelligence were needed to develop a sufficient culture for sheltering members from the harshness of an unkind environment and to invent the tool technologies useful in hunting game. They faced the daunting challenge of creating a radically new form of existence supported by yet-to-be-invented survival strategies. Strong pressures to develop innovative survival skills put a new emphasis on the importance of adapting. The result was that over time physical, mental, and social changes evolved. Their many creative responses to novel challenges were instrumental in the evolution of new levels of intelligence.

In this challenging new environment, the evolution of brain structures and their potential for accommodating new intelligence now exerted strong pressures. The neuron-rich layers of the cerebral cortex were already busy processing the sensory information garnered from the environment and using it to promote survival. The evolution of new neuronal complexity enabled newly evolved capabilities to go beyond immediate survival and to perform mental abstractions like long-range planning and inventive thinking. Human brains slowly acquired a capacity for abstract thought. Creative, mathematical, and musical abilities were cultivated in early humans until today mankind is deciphering the mathematical nature of the universe and standing on the brink of more mental powers.

How were the mental powers for rational and creative thought added to the human intellectual repertoire? They appear to go well beyond the sensory intelligence needed for Darwinian survival. We can only wonder how it came about that cerebral evolution rendered the surprising ability to find patterns in nature and to describe them abstractly in theoretical and mathematical terms. Or conversely, why the design of the cosmos should be such that it is so accessible to functions in the human brain? Recall Einstein's wonder at the fact that the universe is surprisingly comprehensible to the human mind.

The essence of the cosmos is intelligence. The cosmic q-reality acts as the infrastructure supporting development of the universe and generating the intelligence from which life and mind flow. There is a strong possibility that the higher aspect of human intelligence is emulating the order and intelligence contained in the very structure of the universe itself. The human brain has succeeded in capturing a small slice of this colossal intelligence. This should not appear implausible since the very same natural laws and evolutionary processes that put together the universe in the first place have also guided the formation of life and the human brain. Mathematical physicist Paul Davies has said,

> ... *much of the mathematics that is so spectacularly effective in physical theory was worked out as an abstract exercise by pure mathematicians long before it was applied to the real world.*

In other words, in many instances only after formulating their theorems describing how the universe works were scientists able to prove them experimentally. Such a mystifying mental attribute as this makes it necessary to look beyond Darwinian explanations of a sense-oriented brain that evolved millions of years ago for purposes of physical survival.

If purist mathematicians could formulate their theorems first and only later was it discovered that their abstractions actually corresponded with nature, then it is not a stretch to conclude that human brain structures evolved by emulating higher structures of intelligence contained in the very fabric of the universe. We must face the fact that science has not solved the riddle of how or why the human brain *grew* a cerebral cortex so much larger and so much more complex than its nearest earthly relative.

What is responsible for the uncanny human ability to do forms of abstract thinking not directly related to survival? It is difficult to ascribe the mathematical, musical, and creative powers of the brain to a natural extension of basic survival mechanisms developed for processing sensory data from the surrounding environment. Granting that Darwinian evolution adequately explains the neuronal development needed for processing sensory information, further explanations are needed for the new levels of intellect that supply the human mind with the cognitive power to reason, imagine, intuit, and innovate. These are powers well beyond the pale of Darwinian theories of biological evolution. Development of the sensory brain provided a window to the environment enabling survival of those most fit. The huge enlargement of the cerebral part of the brain in humans is providing an altogether different capability.

Taking a closer look at the capabilities of the human brain, it appears there are two independent styles of thinking. One mode of operation involves the manipulation of stored data acquired through the physical senses. Knowledge at this level relates easily to the demands of survival and is covered adequately by the tenets of Darwinian evolution. A second mode for acquiring knowledge of a more abstract nature involves the higher cerebral powers of the brain. Imagination, intuition, rational thinking, and creativity come to us not through the physical senses but more from the internal processing of neuronal networks. Moreover, new evidence points to the strong possibility that the brain does not perform these processing functions unassisted. Perhaps the best explanation at this time is that neuronal networking circuits, working in conjunction with the chakras and aura, produce abstract intelligence by gathering the organization and intelligence found in the universe's q-fields.

The physical structures of the brain provide the hardware. Experience, idea manipulation, and the ability to access higher intelligence write the software. The software then becomes embedded in the hardware by formation of the brain's neuronal networks that act as processing pathways and memory storage. Thus, as the brain's neural organization achieves some degree of similarity with the designs of intelligence in the q-world, mental efficiency increases. In other words, the greater the degree of similarity with quantum order, the greater is the ability of a human brain to tune into the intelligence in the cosmos. The more a brain's structural similarity corresponds with the matrix in the q-reality, the more efficient personal intelligence becomes.

We know from the Uncertainty Principle given in quantum physics that both the momentum and position of an electron cannot be measured simultaneously. Each measurement must be dealt with independently and even then a precise result cannot be attained, only a probability for a range of values. This inexactness defines the nature of activity in open systems and the constant flux of the q-world. The q-world seems to present its tiny inhabitants with behavioral alternatives. A photon of light is sometimes a particle, other times a wave. An individual electron will present its momentum or its position for measurement but never both at the same time. In a real sense, freedom of choice begins in the q-world with certain options for the electron and then extends this openness of choice to ourselves. A similar openness of the neuronal activity in the human brain exists and provides a limited range of behavioral choices. There are not unlimited alternatives available to either the electron or humans, merely a range from which to choose.

When a quantum researcher sets up an experiment, it is the experimenter who determines the values of the initial conditions. These values will define the parameters of the experiment and determine the limited range of alternatives available to a particular electron. Likewise, when the creative intelligence behind the big bang selected very precise values for atomic mass, charge, and force, a narrow range was defined within which matter could evolve. Then, guided by natural law, the evolution of matter proceeded in the direction of organized complexity. During the evolutionary process, there was a window open for the operation of chance and choice. But because of the unchanging laws of physics, chemistry, and the inherent principles of self-organization, evolutionary processes encouraged the cosmos and life to move in the direction of more complexity. If were the initial values were different, life as we know it would not have evolved.

So, if you seek to know the essential nature of the universe, it would be difficult to find a more defining and fundamental characteristic than its intelligence. Natural law is intelligence in action. The settings, constants, forces and natural processes at work in the cosmos have brought, and are bringing, the material universe together in increasingly complex ways. Without the guiding intelligence of natural law, inorganic atoms in the physical universe would never have organized themselves into living organic cells. Without the guiding hand of intelligent rules to follow, the half-dozen or so neurons in early worm brains would never have multiplied, organized, and evolved through the animal kingdom to reach the operational complexity seen in the 100 billion neurons in the modern human brain. Without an intelligent plan, the inexorable progression of sentience would not have moved from a primitive ability to sense light to the phenomenon of mind. And without the inherent element of nature's unrelenting quest to become more complex, and hence intelligent, the 400cc brain of Australopithecus would not have evolved into the 1400cc brain of H. sapiens. The two original tenets of Darwin's theory (survival of the fittest by *random selection* from *physical variations*) are inadequate explanations of the brain's highly ordered neural complexity. What is needed is the addition of nature's inherent drive to follow rules and organize itself in an ever-increasing fashion. In other words, without Mother Nature's innate ability to self-organize in the direction of complexity, we would not be here with an intelligent mind seeking to understand the workings of a super-intelligent *mind-at-large* in the universe.

Traditional doctrine says the brain creates intelligence but pure intelligence must have existed prior to brains since it was intelligence that organized matter to create the brain. It follows then that brains were created by a prior intelligence and that now human brains can act as a focusing device through which this prior intelligence can flow. In other words, the intelligence instilled in natural law set the rules by which physics and chemistry organized the material structures of the brain. From these laws, intelligence emerged through the medium of brains, much like life has emerged through the medium of matter. It may appear that intelligence emanates in and from the brain but the proposed reality is that the brain is a material device through which the vast intelligence contained in the q-world can be narrowed down for use by humans.

It might be argued that the ultimate purpose of a human brain is to achieve intellectual wisdom and a fully enlightened consciousness. The kernel of the brain's essence contains the ingredients needed to achieve this potential. So we must ask why the achievement of this promised potential is still remote. The first response is that we are moving in the right direction, some faster than others. Human intelligence and conscious awareness have progressed in a consistent upward step-function through the corridors of time. Levels of intelligence have made progressive jumps from H. habilis to H. erectus to H. sapiens and this is now reflected clearly in the advancement of a culture that produces new art, science, and technology over time. The second response to why we have not fully reached this potential lies with the vagaries of life. Simply because the ultimate goal of the human brain is to reach some grandiose state does not mean that all will reach it or that this state will be attained at some particular point in time. The probability for success improves as impediments to human development are removed and growth-enhancing conditions are introduced. Not every acorn becomes an oak tree, even though the acorn seed may contain the perfect inner programming needed to realize its potential as an oak tree. Along the way, the vagaries of life can impede or eliminate this realization. A squirrel may have the acorn for lunch or the seed may not find the life-friendly combination of soil, water, and sunlight needed for germination and growth.

So it is with human intellectual development and its nourishment. Genetic inheritance supplies brain structures with some pre-wiring but personal learning experiences are needed to do the further programming for complexity in neural connections. Brain development responds favorably to conditions that are conducive to learning and self-development. As learning proceeds, the density of the brain's neural networking system increases. And the richness of neural interconnections provides increased resonance to connect with the intelligence of highly-ordered q-fields in the universe.

If the cosmos has purpose, and it is hard to believe that its high levels of evolved complexity have happened by chance or for naught, its goal might best be deciphered in the evolving complexity of the human mind. As the brain's organization emulates the intelligence embedded in the cosmos, the intelligence issuing from the brain reflects the nature of the intelligence instilled in the universe.

The process of evolution has taken brain matter to such intricate levels that they now accommodate a mental ability to be participants in their own evolutionary development. In a spacetime universe, matter and mind must interact in order to produce intelligence. This interaction follows the natural laws and principles of self-organization that were activated at the onset of the big bang. Without the universal rules of operation that promote the formation of complexity, the cosmos would be an unstructured and purposeless hodgepodge.

Now, after 14 billion years evolving in spacetime, all the while working under the tutelage of finely-adjusted electrical charges within atoms and adhering unremittingly to the dictates of the four forces, matter has finally gained the organization needed to exhibit the phenomenon of intelligence. We have become empowered by the gift of sufficient intelligence to seek its continued growth by actually joining in the evolutionary process. Heartened by the power of this newfound mental attribute, we have reached a point where human intellectual curiosity enjoins us to ask how this faculty has come about and what is its purpose.

CONCLUSION

Whenever science sufficiently presses, pushes, and tweaks the existing paradigm, it is replaced by a newer one that has been updated with more comprehensive information about the nature of the world we live in. Now, science has uncovered an entirely new and radically different world beneath the level of the atom. In this q-realm of intense activity, there is an organized matrix of intelligence that portends immense importance in the shaping of the universe and how its inhabitants develop and function. The world of the q-reality permeates all of space with cosmic-wide energy fields. It connects all matter in the universe in a single, comprehensive, interactive web-like network. It provides energy and connectivity to and between the material and spiritual worlds. It is ruled by well-ordered data fields instilled in the fabric of the cosmos. Increasingly, this grid of intelligence is being recognized as providing information to the *biofield* that surrounds humans, blending us with our ecologies and uniting us in a web of information that is a cohesive supersystem.

Niels Bohr once remarked that if someone is not *shocked* by the strange behavior of waves and particles in the q-world, then he does not understand quantum physics. Those who have a modicum of understanding of activities in this mysterious realm are stunned by its puzzling contrast with the physical world perceived by our senses. Strange as it may seem to those of us born into a world described in the terms of Newtonian physics, the emerging truth is that our material world is merely a secondary effect arising from the more basic q-reality. Our perceived reality is maya, an illusion that is a mere reflection coming from activity at a more fundamental level. The material world, then, presented to us by our senses flows from the more basic reality found in the q-world.

Transitioning to a new way of looking at the world is not an easy task. A willingness to entertain the possibilities of new and strange sounding ideas cannot co-exist with a blind faith in one of the established dogmas. Dogmatism can infect the thinking of layman, philosopher, and scientist alike, as when strict Darwinists reject the possibility of *intention* in the making of life. Likewise, the religionist who shuns the findings of science limits possibilities for new and more accurate knowledge of the world. So does the scientist who remains fixed upon a particular agenda. In a display of openness to new truths about the world, the Dalai Lama has instructed his followers that when science provides conclusive data that contradicts one of their beliefs, then that belief should be discarded. Remaining open and receptive to the testing of new ideas is critical. New intellectual growth will not come to a locked-in mindset focused on a dogma that claims a certain theory or belief cannot possibly be wrong. Willingness to assimilate new information is key to the promotion of scientific, cultural, and personal growth.

Ancient sages spoke of the world presented to us by our senses as illusion. Now, firmly ensconced in this age of scientific materialism, we are prone to ask if there can be anything more real than solid matter. What if the answer is, *Yes!*? What if the true reality is that solid matter is not solid at all, that it only appears that way to our physical senses. Thousands of years after the introduction of the maya concept, quantum physics is telling us much the same thing. Namely, that the world of our unaided senses reveals only a surface view of the full reality within which we live. Now, we know there is a deeper reality beyond that which we can see or touch and that its intelligence can be tuned in by the aura/brain system and used as an operative force in our lives.

So what is real? Let's take a short trip into the q-world where photons of energy are sometimes waves and other times particles, where an electron will allow you to observe and measure its position *or* its momentum but never both at the same time, where this same electron will move from one place to another without traversing the space in between or consuming time. This is the nature of the q-world from whence emerges the material world perceived by our senses. Though it may be hard to accept, it means that our perceived reality, so full of form and color, is a mere secondary projection of something more basic.

As mentioned, these recent discoveries in quantum physics oddly coincide with the ancient idea that our perceived world is maya. The q-reality is finding agreement with the Eastern teaching that the world we perceive emerges through our consciousness from some deeper reality that may itself be conscious. The introduction of mind and consciousness into physics is an advancement that science has resisted for a long time. Now, the window is opening to the involvement of consciousness not only in the microworld of quantum physics but also in the macroworld of matter.

The combination of powerful magnifying instruments and open scientific minds is demonstrating a totally new and strange foundation from which the material world and life itself emanates. The atom is mostly *empty* space. Even its chief components (nucleus, protons, electrons) are not solid matter but more like small nodes of wave energy. And even they are not fundamental but consist of even smaller parts. Enter, once again, Einstein's finding that energy converts to matter and matter to energy. At the most fundamental level, the universe is a well-ordered energy field saturated with information. And from this foundational field of intelligent energy, the universe evolved life and mind.

More and more scientists are recognizing that an organizing superintelligence inherent within the very nature of the universe brings method from chaos. Some are even accepting the ancient notion of the universe as a living entity. Our difficulty in visualizing the universe as a being lies with the unalterable fact that we are looking at it from the inside. It is as though one cell within a human body attempted to fathom the body's totality from its interior perspective. If we could step beyond space and time and see the universe in the way that our mind can step beyond the body to see it as a living creature, then we might be able to discern an organic nature in the universe. The only escape from this limited perspective lies with the awesome track record of the mind's ability to expand to new dimensions. In its early dimness, mind was merely co-extensive with the body. Over time it expanded beyond the body to encompass the territory within the visible horizon. Later it spread farther to include the stars and galaxies. Now we ask, "Can mind take the next step and expand beyond space and time and enter the causative realm from which our universe emanated?"

Consider the fact that artificial intelligence is modeled after human intelligence. Likewise as it evolves, human intelligence can be viewed as its attempt to model the quantum intelligence structured in the informational fields of the universe. This raises the possibility that the intelligence of the q-world is modeled after an outlying

Supeintelligence beyond the universe and responsible for its origination.

Many scientists find it surprising that we are beginning to better understand the nature of the cosmos. Our growing knowledge of the universe should not be surprising, however, if our intelligence is an emulation of a higher intelligence that exists both within and possibly beyond the universe. If this is the case, then it makes good sense that the universe should begin to look intelligible to us. Even though our emulation of this higher intelligence is still imperfect and woefully incomplete, we may be moving in the right direction and in the process of modeling it. The brain/aura/chakra system acts as a wave receptor interfacing with the q-world. and guiding further development of human intelligence.

A new group promoting the *intelligent design* (ID) of the universe is investigating novel approaches for understanding the development of the cosmos and its life. One contingent of this approach has sprung not from creationists but from scientists who see the presence of far too much complexity of design in the universe for it to have come about by random chance. The intricacies of the genetic code contained in DNA and the complexity of functions in the human brain, they say, could result only from adherence to a system of intelligent laws. These laws lie far beyond the design capability currently seen in humans. Bill Gates, who employs thousands of design engineers and programmers, has likened DNA to his Microsoft programs only that the genetic codes are far more complex than anything his company can produce. The vast array of software programs supporting WORD and WINDOWS could never be punched out by random chance. They have come about only by carefully following an intelligent protocol. The improbability that the high levels of order in the universe and the diversity of its life have resulted accidentally leads ID theorists to assert that there must be intention and purpose behind it all.

In reviewing Paul Davies' *The Fifth Miracle,* Philip Johnson states,

> *If genetic information is comparable to software, it must be designed by an entity with the capability of a software designer.*

While this is true, it should be remembered that software programs run the hardware but software does not build the hardware. The genetic code (software) organizes matter in such a way that bodies and brains (hardware) are intelligently built.

Yes, software runs a computer to reach a goal, (i.e., solve a problem) but what directs the operation of the brain to solve a problem or reach a goal? It is intelligence. Intelligence emerges from a high level of cellular organization in the brain but what directed this organization? It was done by the silent work of natural law as it organized matter in increasingly complex ways.

Futurist and scientist Ray Kurtzweil writes in *The Intelligent Universe*:

> *The universe has been set up in an exquisitely specific way so that evolution could produce the people that are sitting here today and we could use*

our intelligence to talk about the universe. We see
a formidable power in the ability to use our minds
and the tools we've created to gather evidence, to
use our inferential abilities to develop theories, to
test the theories, and to understand the universe at
increasingly precise levels.

Human intelligence, along with its close associates of mind and consciousness, continues to develop even today by emulating the embedded intelligence of the universe's q-fields. In so doing, intelligence seeks, perhaps unwittingly, to reach the ultimate goal of knowing something about the super intelligence that preceded it.

We have witnessed an unstoppable march of sentience from primitive instincts in early animals to current levels of human intelligence. How has this improbable series of events come about? The universe's natural laws, physical constants, and chemical ratios appear pre-arranged with clever foresight so that matter would organize itself into sufficient complexity and bring forth life. The codes of DNA direct many pathways for development and have resulted in life's great diversity of forms. Likewise, the laws and constants of nature guide the development of complexity as they seek continuing order in the formation of matter and mind. In a very real sense, life is the vehicle that accommodates intelligence. As long as life and brains continue to evolve, intelligence will follow suit. The next evolutionary step will be achieved by merging the human aura and chakras with brain and consciousness in a more powerful intellectual system.

While the growth process of intelligence in individuals may be painfully slow, development can be encouraged by the time-honored application of thoughtful study and mindful meditation. Such development, of course, relates to growth within the time frame of an individual lifespan. These techniques, however, promote the expansion of knowledge and collective awareness within the species. Taking the long view, this process of individual efforts seeking knowledge and growth may enable H. sapiens to move beyond the current levels of intelligence and perhaps even attain a new species.

MAY YOU LIVE IN INTERESTING TIMES

Hidden within this ancient Chinese wish is the idea that in order to grow psychologically and intellectually you must encounter crises in your life. If you are willing to confront the difficult challenges of change, then the events of chaos and crisis in your life are in point of fact the presentation of opportunities for growth. According to historian Arnold Toynbee, the cultural advance of civilizations resulted from various groups making positive responses to their survival-threatening challenges. At the level of each individual, while a certain (and debatable) portion of intelligence is genetically established at the moment of conception, much remains for the role of experience in developing the full potential of the intellect. Aided by adequate diet, social interactions, and challenging learning experiences, new neuronal complexity is added to inherited brain structures. Richer development of neuronal networking in the brain occurs when we are confronted by, and then cope with, challenging personal experiences. This is intellectual evolution in action.

As brain complexity increases and begins to resonate more closely with the frequencies of the chakras and aura, there are accompanying increases in the brain's capabilities for tuning in frequencies emanating from the q-world. In turn, this enhanced ability further encourages the development of personal intelligence. Again, this is evolution at work as it propels human intelligence along a developmental path that seeks to emulate a higher order from a universal intelligence. If humans will soon be able to communicate directly with machines via thought,[viii] then it is not a stretch to accept the notion that we can receive communication from the intelligent q-fields of the cosmos. These q-fields, and humans as well, have resulted from the same evolutionary process.

Although in early times the awareness of protohumans was dim and narrow, it has expanded in a step-like fashion until now it incorporates an awareness of the cosmos. As we gain greater recognition of the role that mind and consciousness can play in our lives, awareness expands beyond the personal ego and into the realm of a higher self. Consciousness is our connection to cosmic intelligence. Until recently space was considered a vacuum devoid of energy and matter; however, it is anything but that. The q-fields encompassing all of space are not only a plenum chock-full of energized waveforms but they are a source of intelligence for organizing the tiny particles that combine to constitute the physical world. Moreover, the wave energy emanating from the quantum plenum contains the information needed to mold matter into ever-increasing physical complexity and bio-diversity.

---

viii   Promising development is underway. Communication between electronics and brain neurons has already been demonstrated. Simple computer games can be controlled by human thought via chips that interface directly with the human nerve system.

While the manifest physical world appears to our senses to be the obvious reality, it is the illusion of *maya*. The q-reality is the underlying causative source that forms all the material objects perceived by our senses. We cannot directly perceive the q-world but it is the precursor of all that we do perceive. From the fluctuating q-fields of space, the billions of galaxies with their billions of stars have evolved. And not the least of evolutionary feats is the compact structure of the human brain with its gift for processing information and generating conscious awareness. The human brain working in conjunction with the chakras and the auras is our interface with the wonders of the universe.

Understanding this leads to the realization that the incoming informational sources available to the brain are not limited to the five physical senses. As the mind adapts to the intelligence in the q-fields, we become the recipients of wave energy that the body and brain can convert into thought, imagination, intuition, and emotion. Via the gradual evolution of more complex neuronal structures and better interactive links with the aura, our brains become able to slice off and incorporate in ourselves a part of the order and intelligence from the cosmos. As our consciousness expands beyond the limits of eye and ear sensory information and into the intelligence contained in the universe, we can begin to realize that we are more than biomechanical entities. Not unlike the dynamic and evolving universe itself, we have sprung from the very same sources of energy and superintelligence. We, too, are dynamic, evolving entities. The cosmos is a web-like entity with all of its parts complexly interconnected in a functioning system.

Improving the connection of our consciousness with this higher-level superconsciousness informs us with data from a matrix of cosmic intelligence that enables us to self-organize and self-evolve.

The bottom line is that there is a cosmic-wide field of wave energy carrying information central to all development in the universe. This field of information projects its influence to the development of organic matter and then extends it into the domain of life and mind. It connects not only energy from the q-world with objects in the macroworld but also links human minds with the intelligence of cosmic order. As an ongoing continuation of the evolutionary process, we humans have now developed to a point where we can begin to participate in the process itself. The current evolutionary path seems chiefly focused on the goal of expanding the dimensions of mind.

To further encourage and participate in this ongoing developmental process, it benefits us to understand where and what we have come from and how such knowledge of our origins is of value to the continuation of the evolutionary process. Earlier we sketched how Darwinian evolution provides a basis for understanding how our species coped with the challenges of survival, made adaptations to environmental demands, and in so doing experienced physical modifications, not the least being a phenomenal increase in brain size. But our origins go deeper than Darwinian explanations. They return to the moment of the big bang when space and time began and the rule of natural law commenced.

Quantum physics has revealed that the infrastructure of the universe is a pulsating web of waves charged with energy, the four forces, and information. The q-fields act as a region of influence by mediating activities in the universe. In the q-world tiny *particles* are not so much material as they are minute points of wave energy ceaselessly coming into and moving out of existence. The upshot of this boundless action is that the universe is a vast region of inexhaustible energy and information. So what we have is a universe that at its most elemental level consists of waves carrying energy and encoded with information that is available to us. This is a startlingly different concept from the current world view of Newtonian materialism where the apparent world can be apprehended by our physical senses.

Depending on the orderliness of its structural arrangements, a modern human brain can access information encoded in the q-fields of the universe and transform this received information into a new perception of self and world. This process of acquiring information from the universe via the brain and aura is not entirely dissimilar from how a television set receives electromagnetic waves from a broadcast tower and transforms these waves into a picture on the screen. Our colorful perception of the world exists only inside the brain; outside, all the apparent colors and forms are only clusters of wave energy. Our senses are capable of receiving only waves. We *see* only light waves and then interpret them as colors and forms. The brain can build images and pictures only because the incoming waves are encoded with information. This means that at its most fundamental level, the universe and the world we see are simply waveforms carrying information. To varying degrees, human brains have achieved sufficient complexity to tune into the order and information contained in the primary, q-reality. What we have at our disposal is an information gathering system that acts as a tuned circuit connecting us with the universe and its creative intelligence. This is nothing more and nothing less than an extension of the evolutionary processes that from the very beginning of time have designed the universe by guiding the formation of energy into matter and matter in the direction of mind.

In sharp opposition to the old idea that human brain structures remain fixed after the first few early years of development, neuroscience now recognizes a neuronal plasticity that allows formation of new physical components in the brain. Once again, there is evidence that nature in its unceasing quest to increase complexity continues to evolve a potential for new mental capacities, even in adults. Until recently, it was thought that we were stuck for life with the brain material nature gave us at birth and in the brief explosion of new neurons created in the early years of childhood. Now it appears that new structures and their associated functions can be added to the brain well into adulthood.

This may bring about a major shift in the conventional thinking that increases in brain size precede the expansion of mind. In other words, as brain size increased across the species, expansion of mind and intelligence followed. It was thought that over evolutionary time only trans-species increases in brain size enabled jumps to new levels of intelligence. Opposed to this interpretation it now appears that mind may act as the leading edge and promote the conditions needed for brain-size expansion. Science and the ancient teachings of Buddhism are coming together in the belief that through focused attention, actual structural and functional changes can be created in the brain. This recently recognized capacity opens new vistas for the continuing development of consciousness and intelligence.

The new science of neuroplasticity is telling us that software trumps hardware in the creation of mind. It says that new neurons and brain structures can be formed using the power of mental activity, particularly focused attention in response to challenges. This stunning revelation is liberating us from the old concept of a fixed brain and introducing the revolutionary idea that even in adults new brain material can be created when novel challenges are confronted mindfully. Brains as well as muscles can be augmented through exercise. Changes in brain organization are possible beyond the creation of new neuronal pathways as a result of learning. There are, it turns out, many stem cells in the brain waiting in reserve for the mental challenges that will stimulate and convert these cells into new brain material. This means, quite surprisingly, that new neurons can be made and then organized into new brain structures, thereby creating new mental functions. So if you are not satisfied with the brain you have, you can change it with the focused attention of meditation, or one of the other mindful coping techniques.

To put this idea in a larger perspective, the brain can be viewed as but one of several components in the human intelligence system. The human aura, the chakras, and the q-fields of the cosmos are integral role players in the informational system that supports the brain and creates mind. With assistance from the aura and chakras, the brain accesses the q-fields and together these components form an informational system that provides the intelligence we use in creating our lives and designing the culture in which we live.

We are beginning to get our mental arms around some far-reaching concepts. And like the early human prototypes that felt coextensive only with the limited range of their trekking grounds, we now somehow feel an identity, even a destiny, with the entire universe. Early humans moved out of their homelands and survived by adapting to the environmental features of the new territories. In so doing, it molded their physical and mental evolution. Likewise, we are now using our minds to move into new intellectual territory and open cosmic vistas that will encourage and guide the future evolution of intelligence and consciousness. We can see this type of evolution at work in our personal lives. We use our minds to open up new evolutionary space via dreams and goals and then by dent of mindful effort move our personal reality into this new mental territory. In the process, consciousness expands. Some philosophical thinkers like Teilhard de Chardin claim that all of evolution has been an inevitable ascent toward increased consciousness and eventually super consciousness.

How is it possible to use our minds to open new mental realms into which we can evolve? Even though we use abstract terms like intention, motivation, diligence and intelligence to explain our achievements, we still do not know definitively what consciousness is or why it even exists. What early survival advantage did consciousness provide? Within the processing system of the brain, there is a mix of everyday perceptual inputs from our five physical senses and this mixture ignites neuronal firings that correlate with our inner sense of conscious awareness. But how do inputs from the physical senses generate the wide range of emotional feelings associated with our consciousness?

At some point in the evolutionary process, humans became aware of themselves as members of a society as well as possessing an identity as individuals. They came to view themselves as situated in an earthly environment that is part of a planetary system in a universe of incredible size and grandeur. Following birth, each of us experiences a similar and presaging awakening of consciousness but in a very private and highly personalized way. We slowly learn to differentiate our youthful bodies from our mothers and then from the surrounding environment. Eventually, we come to see ourselves as distinct and independent streams of consciousness within a larger social context. Moreover, we are not only aware of this awakening of consciousness but we also become aware that we are aware of it. On this planet, humans are the ultimate achievement in self-reflective consciousness.

It is difficult to explain how attributes like subjective emotions, abstract concepts like the *self,* and such private experiences as wonder, pain, guilt and love began their emergence from arrangements of physical matter in the bodies and brains of protohumans. The material in our brains is constituted of the very same atoms and molecules from the earth's crust that make up rocks and worms? Can something so immaterial and ethereal, so exquisite and tenuous as the flow of consciousness arise from the interplay of tiny bits of organized matter? How do the electrical oscillations of firing nerve cells in the brain give birth to the private sensations of conscience, guilt, and shame? Can patterns of neuronal excitation really create emotional experiences like the exquisite contentment of a accomplishment or feelings of joy and sorrow? Is the organization of neural material in a stand-alone brain sufficient in and of itself to create the elegance of abstract thinking, mathematics, and creative imagination?

We are on the cusp of a new assimilation that will vastly increase our intelligence. As the aura and chakras become better integrated with brain functions, a new intelligence system will open more of the exquisite wonders of the universe and our own nature. Back in evolutionary time when the mammalian brain was first integrated with the older reptilian nodule, an array of new mental features appeared. Later, the addition of the cerebral cortex to the two older brain modules opened for mankind previously unfathomed opportunities via new brain functions. Who can say where the next system upgrade will lead us when the introduction of the chakras and aura becomes more fully integrated with the material functions of the brain?

WRAP-UP

While not a scientist in a professional sense, my inclination has been to rely on scientific thinking and seek verifiable information to construct a good part of my belief system. I am comfortable with an evolutionary process that has brought together subatomic matter to make living cells, organs, bodies, and brains. This does not preclude the putative necessity for a Source responsible for putting together natural law and the rules of operation that have guided this awe-inspiring evolution. I am not, however, at ease with the strict scientist's tenet that my subjective world of thought, dreams, emotions, goals and motivations can be reduced mechanistically to the activities of matter in a stand-alone brain. Scientific materialism has not appeased a certain doubt about its contention that matter is the prime mover in the universe and that it alone can substantiate all that I think, feel and intuit. The intellectual phenom, Stephen Hawking, has said there must be something that breathes fire into his equations. And for me there seems to be something beyond a material body and the neurons in my brain that breathes animation and spirit into my constructed reality.

As I peer outward from the cranial brain vault that encapsulates my inside world and consider the vast cosmic Superintelligence that has shaped the expansive outside world, I realize that I myself am a small result of the same intelligence that has constructed the universe. Atoms did not gather themselves by random chance to construct such an orderly and magnificent universe. Natural laws did not magically write themselves by random chance to direct the evolutionary process as it developed the universe and its life. The embryonic level of human intelligence is a work-in-process as it attempts to copy the majesty of cosmic intelligence. The current conclusions of science and psychology - frequently contradictory and often revised - do not satisfy a nagging compulsion to understand the reality of the inner and outer worlds. In response to this abiding curiosity, some seek comfort from the angst of uncertainty in the refuge of belief in a powerful and benign deity. Yet, to the scientifically inclined this seems to be a surrender to the notion that the recondite phenomena of the natural world are beyond the pale of human understanding. Better, it seems, to follow the natural curiosity instilled in the human intellect and seek to resolve these remaining untamed phenomena by dint of intellectual effort.

So now we come to a final consideration of the ever-evolving natural phenomenon of intelligence, a constant companion with development in human life. We know much about the cosmos and how it has been built tiny particle by tiny particle into galaxies, stars, and planets. The subjectivity of mind and consciousness, however, has not easily yielded to scientific investigation. Both remain elusive and resistant to full explanation. Even though we know much about the physical world, it seems next to impossible to substantiate conclusively the notion that the primary nature of the universe is exclusively material. Something more than the undirected activities of matter alone have guided formation of the complex arrangements that have resulted in life, mind and consciousness. There must be some sort of cosmic-wide super intelligence guiding development not only of matter but also the nonmaterial aspect of the universe.

In addition to the revelations coming from q-physics and our own inner insight, perhaps the closest we have come to supporting the concept of a nonmaterial nature in the universe rests with the ever-increasing occurrence and documentation of human near death experiences (NDEs). Modern medical equipment has increased the number of resuscitations of clinically *dead* patients. There are striking similarities in the reported accounts of these survivors. Emerging is the common theme of visiting a very different world, meeting deceased friends, relatives and beings of light, and all the while experiencing a high level of warmth and elation. Most of these *deceased* patients did not wish to return to *life* and those who do undergo radical changes in lifestyle characterized by less ego centricity and a loss of the fear for death.

Some researchers see NDE's as early evidence that consciousness is not dependent for its existence on brain matter and that personal awareness continues after the brain flat-lines. The information culled from NDE experiences is somewhat akin to the ideas of Aldous Huxley in that brains function as a *reducing valve* to *protect* us from too much cosmic input. Think of the brain as a screening organ that permits us to be aware of only small amounts of the massive store of intelligence within the q-reality. When brain function ceases, awareness and the personal data store of the aura continue. The nature of the q-reality, combined with the findings of NDE research, tend to support a universe possessing both material and nonmaterial qualities.

Dreams during normal sleep do not exhibit the trans-personal similarities of NDEs. It is interesting to note that in normal sleep we dream of both the living and deceased while NDEs mention encountering only those who are deceased. If accounts of NDE's are not actual occurrences of consciousness surviving a brain-dead body, it leads to the surmise that human brains must be hard-wired to produce a hallucinatory experience with spiritual undertones in the event of an extreme circumstance. Some NDEs are joyful, life-enhancing experiences; others are fearful, even terrifying. If NDEs are not indicative of the survival of consciousness following death of the body, then the source of this experience must come from an innate structure residing somewhere in the human brain. It then becomes necessary to explain the appearance of such an unusual structure from an evolutionary perspective. This is a tall task for a Darwinian process that evolved during the Pleistocene to promote survival of the species by selecting for fitness with that early environment.

This leads to renewal of the old and fruitful but still unresolved debate between strict scientific materialists and those who see a nonmaterial content in the universe. It is a dispute that has proliferated across many disciplines, infiltrating and fertilizing a number of intellectual fields. One of the most productive exchanges has been between entrenched Darwinists and upstart intelligent design advocates. The Darwinians see the role of science as a challenge to unravel nature's mysteries without recourse to the intervention of an outside intelligent source. Richard Dawkins is the current outspoken champion of materialism and atheism. In his book *The Blind Watchmaker* he asserts that:

All appearances to the contrary, the only watchmaker in nature is the blind forces of physics …[Darwin"s] natural selection is the blind watchmaker, blind because it does not see ahead, does not plan consequences, has no purpose in view. It has no vision, no foresight, no sight at all.

As a biologist, Dawkins admits that within each one of the trillions of human cells there is

> *... a digitally coded database larger in information content than all 30 volumes of the Encyclopedia Britannica.*

But as a committed materialist he sees this intricate cellular matrix of coded intelligence as the evolved result of countless unplanned interactions between chance and natural law. His claim is that Darwin's principles of natural selection acting on mutational variations suffice in explaining cellular complexity and its resultant diversity of life. In other words, mutation, operating as chance, along with natural law empowered the environment to select those physical characteristics best suited to promote the growth of such complexity.

The current debate between Darwinists and ID-ists is not exactly the old argument between materialism and dualism in that this modern version of non-materialism (ID) has shifted to a more scientific base. Mind and matter are seen as interactive and merely different manifestations of the same energy source.

The scientific component of modern ID theory comes not from a religious agenda but from a quest by scientists for a deeper and more rational explanation of natural phenomena. The orderliness in the universe and the complexity of its life have compelled ID scientists to conclude that such high levels of organization could result only from an intelligent protocol that governed the development of matter. Hence, it implies the need for a first Cause. This leads some to conclude that ID is just another offshoot of creationism. In point of fact, the scientific component of ID has emerged from an integration of quantum physics, chaos theory, and the evolutionary powers of natural law.

A number of disciplines have integrated their ideas to present an updated view of a dynamic and evolving world driven by cosmic energy and guided by the intelligence of an unfolding natural law that issues from the very fabric of the universe. According to this view, life and mind have not evolved randomly from a material base but rather under the direction of an organized intelligence contained in cosmic fields of information. At long last, this integration of ideas may provide an opportunity to find resolution of the competing concepts of materialism and mind. The extreme advocates on each side profess exclusivity for their position as the primary mover of development in the universe. One sees matter as fundamental; the other with a more spiritual content purports mind as something eerily independent of matter.

The new science of complexity is gathering data to further explain the relationship between brain (matter) and mind (spirit) from a base of scientific data. Inherent in the confliction of ideas about the primacy of either matter or mind is the question of which provides the impetus that drives development in the universe. Can matter organize itself sufficiently to create mind and intelligence? The workings of mind, then, would be epiphenomenal, or the mere byproducts of physical and chemical activities. This would crown matter as the prime mover in an evolving world.

On the other hand, if the material brain does not do *all* of its work as a stand-alone device but gets assistance by tapping into the universal grid of intelligence, or Supermind, then matter is not primary. It needs help from the nonmaterial component of mind. Granted that since early evolutionary times brains have learned to process sensory inputs in order to receive vital information about the environment. But the modern human brain does much more. Cerebral operations produce the dazzling and highly abstract outputs of mathematics, science, art and the humanities, as well as such intangibles as wonder, imagination, joy, and creativity. These mental fabrications, along with a complex array of emotions, are better explained by the brain's role as part of a larger system of intelligence. In conjunction with the chakras and the aura, the human brain receives and emulates patterns of intelligence and consciousness from data fields in the cosmic matrix.

The theories of complexity and chaos willingly concede that the brain is a focal point for the emergence of mind and consciousness. The intricately organized material in the brain serves as the infrastructure for many phenomena. Such functions in the brain are capable of producing new phenomena not contained in the operation of any individual neuron. In other words, novel functions are created at higher system levels due to the *interaction* of lower-level components. The simple example of combining two atoms of hydrogen with one atom of oxygen to produce water illustrates how totally new features can appear at higher system levels. Water does not exist in either of the two elements of the compound. The brain's marvelous ability to produce novel effects notwithstanding, we are reaching a point of understanding that supersedes the traditional dogma that has treated intelligence as emerging from the activities of matter alone. The neurons of the brain do combine in complex ways to produce copious outputs from the sensory inputs they monitor in the outside world but mounting evidence is demonstrating the brain to be more than a sensory-driven organ.

The more complex that neural networking becomes, the better brains are able to integrate non-sensory data. The full phenomena of mind, its creativity, imagination, and wondrous abstract abilities, come about with outside assistance. With help from newly developed and highly sensitive energy-detecting instruments, we can now view the brain as one unit in a larger system. The brain, assisted by the body's chakras and aura, is now seen as a receiving organ that picks up waves of intelligence from the matrix grid. From this higher-level system, a more efficient and powerful human intelligence is emerging. The closer the sub-system of brain/aura/chakra emulates the organization of the higher system of intelligence instilled in the universe, the more receptive it becomes at receiving and processing information from this source.

We are conditioned to think of intelligence as more or less hard-wired in the brain with some amount of increase garnered from social and learning experiences during the early years of life. We enter the world with brain structures designed in very early evolutionary times designed for processing sensory inputs from the environment. We further develop and fine-tune these structures to a particular conformation when new neural networks are added as a result of specific environmental experiences. As this process proceeds toward more brain complexity, a protective filter slowly relaxes to allow measured amounts of cosmic consciousness and intelligence to enter. If the filter is opened too wide or too soon, overload problems occur.

Hence, the integrity of human consciousness, and its constant companion intelligence, is maintained by allowing only limited amounts of information from the matrix grid to enter. But as neural complexity increases we gain an ability to tune into more of the super intelligence contained in the matrix fields. (Some theorists claim that when the brain flat- lines and a near death experience occurs this protective filter is removed, thereby allowing consciousness to expand closer to cosmic levels.)

All of this, then, begs the question of an originating Source for the intelligence that is sewn into the fabric of the universe and is being made available to us. Using an imperfect analogy, it can be argued that if the development of the software for WORD and WINDOWS required a Bill Gates, then the software package that we know as natural law also required a Program Designer.

A fundamental question is whether natural law has unfolded randomly in the universe or whether it was *programmed* purposefully. Some strict materialists claim natural law evolved randomly, as did life. Whatever its source, within natural law there is a silent subroutine that nudges the formation of matter in the direction of increasing complexity. This ensures that higher levels of organization will be achieved and new degrees of intelligence will be realized. Life and intelligence are the happy and astonishing consequences of this subtlety in the code of natural law as it ceaselessly seeks to enhance order and complexity. And now this organized *complexification* (Teilhard's word) has led to beings that can use their evolved intelligence to look outward and inward, marveling as they seek to more fully understand the power and source of natural law and the grandeur of its creativity.

Without fanfare, natural law has orchestrated a universe with order, beauty and intelligence. This is what bemused Einstein when he expressed amazement at the harmony of the universe and said that natural law:

> *reveals an intelligence of such superiority that, compared with it, all systematic thinking of human beings is an utterly insignificant reflection.*

And this is what complexity theorist Kaufmann meant when, in reference to the results issuing from the workings of natural law, said, *we the expected*. As humans, we can now visualize ourselves as an integral part of an intelligent system that was preceded by an embryonic idea in an Original Source. That idea led to the creation of a universe which, given sufficient time, has produced us. And as we humans look outward and marvel at the wonders of this universe, we find ourselves looking inward for answers to the riddles of self and the purpose of the cosmos.

What did the Creator have in mind? Go figure.

BIBLIOGRAPHY

Anastasia, Anne, *Psychological Testing,* Macmillan, New York, NY, 1982.

Anastasia, Anne, *Intelligence as a Quality of Behavior in What is Intelligence?: Contemporary Viewpoints on Its Nature and Definition,* R.J. Sternberg and D.K. Letterman (ED.), Able Publishing Corp., Norwood, NJ, 1986.

Arntz, William, *What the Bleep Do We Know!?: Decoding Endless Possibilities For Altering Your Reality* Health Communications, Inc. Deerfield Beach, Fl. 2005.

Barrow, John D. and Tipler, Frank J. *The Anthropic Cosmological Principle,* 1988 Bloom, Howard, *Global Brain,* John Wiley & Sons, Inc. New York, 2000.

Bohm, David, *Wholeness and the Implicate Order.* Routledge and Kegans, Boston, Ma, 1980.

Capra, Fritjof, *The Web of Life.* Anchor Books - Doubleday, NY, 1996.

Davies, Paul, The Mind of God: A Scientific Basis for a Rational World, Simon and Schuster, NY, 1992.

Davies, Paul, *The Fifth Miracle: The Search of the Origin of Life, Simon and Schuster, NY, 1999.*

Dawkins, Richard, *The Blind Watchmaker,* W.W. Norton, NY, 1987.

Dennett, Daniel, *Consciousness Explained,* Little, Brown & Co. Boston, 1991.

Eccles, John C., *Evolution of the Brain: Creation of Self,* Routledge, NY, 1989.

Falk, Dean, *Braindance,* Henry Holt and Company, Inc., NY, 1990.

Flavell, John, *The Development Psychology of Jean Piaget* Van Nostrand, Princeton, NJ, 1963.

Gardner, James, *Biocosm,* Inner Ocean Publishing Inc., Makawao, Maui, Hi, 2003.

Gardner, James, (Author), Kruzweil, Ray (Foreword) *The Intelligent Universe, ET and the Emerging Mind of the Cosmos,* Career Press, Inc. Franklin Lakes, NJ, 2007.

Harth, Erich, *The Creative Loop: How the Brain Makes a Mind,* Addison-Wesley, Reading, Ma. 1993.

Herrnstein, Richard and Murray, Charles, *The Bell Curve: Intelligence and Class Structure in American Life* The Free Press, New York, 1994.

Hoyle, Fred, *The Intelligent Universe,* Michael Joseph, London, 1983.

Hunt, Valerie, *Infinite Mind: Science of Human Vibrations of Consciousness,* Malibu Publishing Co., 1996

Itzkoff, Seymour, *Triumph of the Intelligence,* Paideia, Ashfield, Ma., 1985.

Jantsch, Erich, *The Self-Organizing Universe: Scientific and Human Implications of the Emerging Paradigm of Evolution,* Pergamon Press, NY, 1980.

Jerrison, Harry, *The Evolution of the Brain and Intelligence*, Academic Press, New York, NY, 1973.

Kauffman, Stuart, *At Home in the Universe: The Search for Self-Organization and Complexity.* Oxford University Press, NY, 1995.

Laszlo, Ervin, *Evolution: The Grand Synthesis.* Shambhala Publications, Inc., Boston, MA., 1987.

Mackintosh, Nicholas, *Intelligence in Evolution* in *What is Intelligence?*, Khalfa, Jean (Ed.), Cambridge University Press, New York, NY, 1993.

McTaggart, Lynne, *The Field: A Quest for the Secret Force of the Universe,* Harper Collins, New York, 2002.

Mindell, Arnold, *Quantum Mind,* Lao Tse Press, Portland, Oregon, 2000.

Monod, Jacques, *Chance and Necessity,* Collins, London, 1972.

Morris, Richard, *The Edges of Science,* Simon & Schuster, NY, 1990.

Ornstein, Robert, *The Evolution of Consciousness,* Prentice Hall, NY, 1991.

Pribram, Karl, *Subatomic Physics: Model for Consciousness.* Brain/Mind Bulletin, V.7, No. 10, 1982.

Prigogine, Ilya, *Order Through Fluctuation: Self-Organization and Social System* in Evolution and Consciousness. Editors: E. Jantsch and C. Waddington, Addison-Wesley, Reading, Mass., 1976.

Prigogine, Ilya and Stengers, Isabelle, *Order out of Chaos.* Bantam, New York, 1984.

Richardson, Ken, *The Making of Intelligence,* Columbia University Press, New York, 2000.

Riordan, M., and Schramm, D., *The Shadows of Creation: Dark Matter and the Structure of the Universe,* Freeman Press, NY, 1994.

Sagan, Carl, *The Dragons of Eden: Speculations on the Evolution of Human Intelligence,* Random House, NY, 1977.

Stanley, Steven, *Children of the Ice Age,* Harmony Books, NY, 1996.

Stenhouse, David, *The Evolution of Intelligence: A General Theory and Some of Its Implications,* Barnes and Noble Books, New York, NY, 1974.

Sternberg, Robert, Kaufman, James, *The Evolution of Intelligence,* Lawrence Erlbaum Associates, Publishers, Mahwah, NJ, 2002.

Teilhard de Chardin, Pierre, *The Phenomenon of Man,* Harper and Row, NY, 1965.

Wade, Jenny, *Changes of Mind: A Holonomic Theory of the Evolution of Consciousness,* State University of New York Press, Albany, NY, 1996.

Waldrop, M. Mitchell, *Complexity: The Emerging Science a the Edge of Order and Chaos,* Simon and Shuster, New York, 1992.

White, John, Editor, *Kundalini, Evolution and Enlightenment,* Anchor Books, Garden City, NY, 1979.

Wilber, Ken, *Up From Eden, A Transpersonal View of Human Evolution,* New Science Library, Shambhala, Boston, Ma, 1986.

Wilber, Ken (Ed.), *The Holographic Paradigm and Other Paradoxes,* New Science Library, Boulder, Co, 1982.

Wills, Christopher, *The Runaway Brain,* Basic Books, NY, 1993.

Wolf, Fred Alan, *The Spiritual Universe: How Quantum Physics Proves the Existence of the Soul,* Simon and Shuster, New York, 1996.